NATIONAL GEOGRAPHIC LEARNING

OUTCOMES

INTERMEDIATE
SPLIT A EDITION
STUDENT'S BOOK

HUGH DELLAR
ANDREW WALKLEY

Split Edition A

1 FIRST CLASS

IN THIS UNIT YOU LEARN HOW TO:
- say more about yourself and other people
- ask and answer common questions
- ask follow-up questions and maintain conversations
- describe how well you use different languages
- pay more attention to the language in texts
- tell better stories

page 6

2 FEELINGS

- talk about how you feel – and why
- respond to good and bad news
- talk about your life now
- explain why you can't – or don't want to – do things

page 14

VIDEO 1: Kenya comes to Central Park page 22 REVIEW 1: page 23 WRITING 1: Keeping in touch page 78

3 TIME OFF

- describe places and explain where they are
- give and respond to suggestions
- discuss future plans
- talk about the weather
- recognise and reuse useful chunks of language
- ask and talk about holiday experiences

page 24

4 INTERESTS

- talk about free-time activities
- describe how often you do (or did) things
- explain how good you are at things
- talk about injuries and sports problems
- ask about tastes

page 32

VIDEO 2: World Heritage quiz page 40 REVIEW 2: page 41 WRITING 2: Short emails page 80

5 WORKING LIFE

- talk about jobs and what they involve
- comment on people's experiences
- discuss rules and freedoms at work
- talk about getting used to changes
- say longer chunks better

page 42

6 BUYING AND SELLING

- talk about phones and phone companies
- compare products
- describe what people are wearing
- discuss shopping habits
- describe souvenirs and presents
- negotiate a good price

page 50

VIDEO 3: Wheelin' and dealin' antiques page 58 REVIEW 3: page 59 WRITING 3: Stories page 82

7 EDUCATION

- describe courses, schools, teachers and students
- show you believe or sympathise with what people tell you
- talk about different education systems
- talk about possible future plans or situations
- discuss different aspects of education
- form and say different words from the same root

page 60

8 EATING

- describe different dishes and ways of cooking food
- explain what is on a menu
- discuss experiences of foreign food
- make generalisations
- describe restaurants

page 68

VIDEO 4: The business of cranberries page 76 REVIEW 4: page 77 WRITING 4: Making requests page 84

GRAMMAR	VOCABULARY	READING	LISTENING	DEVELOPING CONVERSATIONS
• Auxiliary verbs • Narrative tenses	• Talking about people • Talking about languages	• The Google translators in human form	• Meeting for the first time • Stories connected to speaking a foreign language	• Asking follow-up questions
• Linking verbs • Present simple and present continuous	• Feelings • **Understanding vocabulary:** -ed / -ing adjectives	• It only takes Juan Mann to change the world!	• Talking about feelings • Juan Mann • Bumping into an old school friend	• Response expressions
• Future plans • Present perfect simple	• Places of interest • Weather • **Understanding vocabulary:** Useful chunks in texts	• Kraków: Places to visit • Is disaster tourism such a total disaster?	• Visiting Kraków • Holiday plans	• Giving and responding to suggestions
• Habit and frequency • Present perfect continuous and past simple for duration	• Free-time activities • Injuries and problems • Describing music	• The playlist of your life	• Free-time activities • Hidden talent	• *Are you any good?* • Talking about tastes
• *Must* and *can't* for commenting • Talking about rules	• Describing jobs • Work rules and laws • **Understanding vocabulary:** *Be used to* and *get used to*	• Terrible jobs not a thing of the past	• Talking about work • Rules at work	• *Doing what?*
• Comparisons • Noun phrases	• Smartphones • Clothes and accessories • Describing souvenirs and presents	• Shop till you drop!	• In a phone shop • Talking about gifts	• Avoiding repetition • Negotiating prices
• Future time clauses • Zero and first conditionals	• Describing courses • Education • **Understanding vocabulary:** Forming words	• What works in education	• Talking about a course • Talking about education	• *I can imagine*, *I bet*, etc.
• Generalisations and *tend to* • Second conditionals	• Describing food • Restaurants	• Food for thought	• In a Peruvian restaurant • Talking about restaurants	• Describing dishes

Grammar reference pages 86–96   Information files pages 97–102   Audio scripts pages 104–113

Contents 3

Split Edition B

IN THIS UNIT YOU LEARN HOW TO:

9 HOUSES
- describe flats, houses and areas
- explain how big places are
- discuss social and economic changes
- compare the past and now
- ask about house rules

10 GOING OUT
- talk about exhibitions, films and the theatre
- explain exactly where places are
- discuss nights out
- use idioms connected to different parts of the body
- describe different kinds of events
- talk about plans that failed to happen and explain why

VIDEO 5: One woman's choice   REVIEW 5   WRITING 5: Formal emails

11 THE NATURAL WORLD
- tell and participate in telling stories
- describe animals
- show emotions through pronunciation
- talk about challenges and achievements
- discuss natural resources and the economy

12 PEOPLE I KNOW
- describe character
- talk about your friends and family
- explain how people you know are similar
- talk about memories
- express regrets
- talk about relationships

VIDEO 6: Greatest journey   REVIEW 6   WRITING 6: Reports

13 JOURNEYS
- talk about journeys
- explain travel problems
- discuss immigration
- reflect on past events
- use extreme adjectives to make descriptions more interesting
- talk about problems and whose fault they are

14 TECHNOLOGY
- talk about computers
- explain and sort out problems
- describe games
- discuss issues around computer gaming
- talk about apps and gadgets

VIDEO 7: Air pollution tracking   REVIEW 7   WRITING 7: Opinion-led essays

15 INJURIES AND ILLNESS
- talk about injuries and illness with a doctor
- discuss health myths and facts
- talk about causes and results
- tell stories about accidents
- report what people said

16 NEWS AND EVENTS
- talk about types and sources of news
- comment on the news
- use reporting verbs to report news
- describe famous people and events
- discuss issues around fame

VIDEO 8: Bee therapy   REVIEW 8   WRITING 8: Reviews

GRAMMAR	VOCABULARY	READING	LISTENING	DEVELOPING CONVERSATIONS
• Present perfect simple and present perfect continuous • Comparing now and the past	• Describing homes • Social issues • Describing areas	• Waiting for the bubble to burst • Small ads	• A new apartment • Room to rent in Berlin	• Explaining how big a place is • Asking about rules
• Quantifiers • The future in the past	• Exhibitions, films and theatre • **Understanding vocabulary:** Idioms • Describing events	• Big night out	• Going to the cinema • What did you do last night?	• Explaining where places are
• Past ability / obligation • Passives	• Movements and sounds • Challenges and achievements	• The strange story of Maurice Wilson • Natural resources fact file	• Animal stories • Maurice Wilson • The resource curse	• Helping people to tell stories
• *Used to*, *would* and past simple • Expressing regret using *wish*	• Describing character • Relationships	• Struggling to fit into the role of granny	• Talking about family • Talking about Nicolas	• *That's like ...*
• Third conditionals • *Should have*	• Ways of travelling and travel problems • **Understanding vocabulary:** Phrasal verbs • **Understanding vocabulary:** Extreme adjectives	• The long journey to a new life	• Talking about journeys • Holiday problems	• *How come?* • Blaming people
• Articles • Infinitive and *-ing* forms	• Computers • Describing games • Apps and gadgets	• My life as a gamer	• IT help desk • The gaming industry • Totally great or total rubbish?	• Sorting out problems
• Adverbs • Reported speech	• Injuries and illness • **Understanding vocabulary:** Word endings and word class • Accidents and health problems	• Fact or myth?	• At the hospital • Accident on holiday	• Short questions with *any*
• Reporting verbs • Defining relative clauses	• News • Explaining who people are	• Seeking fame and fortune	• Talking about news stories • Talking about famous people	• Introducing and commenting on news

Contents 5

1

FIRST CLASS

IN THIS UNIT YOU LEARN HOW TO:

- say more about yourself and other people
- ask and answer common questions
- ask follow-up questions and maintain conversations
- describe how well you use different languages
- pay more attention to the language in texts
- tell better stories

SPEAKING

1 **Work in pairs. Discuss the questions.**
   - Look at the photo of a language class. What do you think is happening?
   - Where do you think it was taken?
   - What do you think they're learning?
   - Would you like to have a class like this? Why? / Why not?

2 **Work with a new partner. Discuss the questions.**
   - Why are you learning English?
   - What English classes have you done before?
   - Do you know anyone in this class?
   - Are you still friends with people from previous classes? Tell your partner as much as you can about each person.

Unit 1   First class   7

NICE TO MEET YOU

LISTENING

1 ▶1 Listen to two conversations in which people meet for the first time. Answer the questions for each conversation.

1 Where do they meet?
2 Why are they there?

2 ▶1 Work in pairs. Try to answer the questions below. Then listen again and check your answers.

Conversation 1
1 How is Alfie feeling? Why?
2 Is Holly a new student?
3 When did Alfie start studying French?
4 What does he think his strengths and weaknesses are?
5 According to Holly, where is French an official language?

Conversation 2
6 How did Noah feel about the talk he attended?
7 Where is Noah from – and where is he living now?
8 When did Noah move to his current home?
9 Has Giuliana visited the city Noah is living in?
10 What does Noah do for a living?

3 With your partner, take turns to tell each other as much as you can about the last new person you met.

VOCABULARY Talking about people

4 Check you understand the words in bold in the sentences below. Then decide which two words / phrases in the box could replace each word / phrase in bold so you are talking about the same subject. The first one is done for you.

Portugese	Japan	an only child	sport
a civil servant	married	reading	a translator
Economics	Medicine	Arabic	a twin
Germany	an office	separated	a warehouse

1 My friend Marcin is from **Poland**.   *Japan, Germany*
2 My husband's **a software engineer**.
3 My brother works in **a university**.
4 My mum speaks good French and a bit of **Russian**.
5 My sister's doing a degree in **Law** at the moment.
6 My parents are really into **travelling**.
7 My friend Imke is **the youngest of six kids.**
8 My aunt Maria is **single**.

5 Think of one more word or phrase that could replace each word / phrase in bold.

6 Work in groups. Use language from Exercises 4 and 5 to say five true things about people you know.

GRAMMAR

Auxiliary verbs

When we make questions and negatives, we use different auxiliary verbs. There are only three: *be*, *do* and *have*.

I **don't** know. (present simple)

How**'s** it going? (present continuous)

Have you been there? (present perfect simple)

7 Look at these questions from the conversations. Then work in pairs and answer the questions below.

a **Do** you know it?
b **Did** you enjoy it?
c **Have** you studied here before?
d Where **are** you based?
e What **are** you doing there? **Are** you working?
f How long have you **been** learning French?

1 Which auxiliary goes with the infinitive (without *to*)?
2 Which two auxiliaries go with the past participle (often an *-ed* form) of the verb?
3 Which auxiliary goes with the *-ing* form of the verb?

Ⓖ Check your ideas on page 86 and do Exercise 1.

PRONUNCIATION

8 ▶2 Listen to the questions from Exercise 7 – first said slowly and then faster. Notice that in faster speech, the auxiliary verbs are hardly heard at all.

9 ▶3 Listen again to the faster version. Practise saying the questions as quickly as you can.

10 Complete the questions with the correct auxiliary verbs.

1 Where _____ you live?
2 Who _____ you live with?
3 How long have you _____ living there?
4 Where _____ you born?
5 How long _____ it usually take you to get to work / school?
6 What _____ you do last weekend? Anything interesting?
7 Why _____ you studying at this school?
8 _____ you ever been to an English-speaking country?
9 _____ anyone else in your family speak English?
10 _____ anyone you know ever lived abroad? Where?

11 Work in pairs. Ask and answer the questions in Exercise 10.

Ⓖ For further practice, see Exercise 2 on page 86.

DEVELOPING CONVERSATIONS

Asking follow-up questions

After someone answers a question we have asked, we often ask a second related question. This helps us to find out more details and to keep the conversation going.

A: So **have you studied here before?**
B: Yeah, last term.
A: Oh really? OK. **And did you enjoy it?**
B: Yeah, it was amazing.

12 Match the questions (1–6) with the pairs of possible follow-up questions (a–f).

1 What are you studying?
2 Have you studied here before?
3 What do you do when you're not studying?
4 Do you have any brothers or sisters?
5 What did you do at the weekend?
6 What do you do?

a Whose class were you in? / Where did you learn your English?
b What year are you in? / What does that involve?
c Older or younger? / What do they do?
d Where do you work? / Do you enjoy it?
e How often do you do that? / Did you get anything nice?
f How long have you been doing that? / What kind of music are you into?

13 Write one more follow-up question you might ask after someone answers questions 1–6 in Exercise 12.

14 ▶4 Listen to six short conversations. What follow-up questions do you hear?

CONVERSATION PRACTICE

15 Choose six questions from this lesson that you think are good to ask people when you first meet them. Then think of two other questions you could also ask.

16 Choose one of these tasks.

a Work with the whole class and have conversations to get to know other students.
b Imagine you are at a party for language students. Look at File 1 on page 97. Choose a person to pretend to be. Then have conversations to get to know other people. Ask and answer questions in the role of the person you chose.

🎥 1 To watch the video and do the activities, see the DVD ROM.

Unit 1 First class 9

TALKING MY LANGUAGE

VOCABULARY Talking about languages

1 Work in pairs. How many of the languages in the picture do you recognise?

2 Complete the sentences about using foreign languages with these words and phrases.

| accent | express | fluently | picked it up |
| accurate | get by | mastering | struggled |

1 I'm not very _____ , but I can hold a conversation and make myself understood.
2 I know the basics – enough to _____ when I'm travelling there.
3 I really _____ with French when I was at school, so I just gave up.
4 I get frustrated when I can't _____ myself.
5 I never went to class. I just _____ from talking to people.
6 I'm a bit embarrassed to speak sometimes because I know I have a strong _____ .
7 I grew up bilingual so I speak Spanish and Japanese _____ .
8 I'm not interested in _____ the language, I just want to be able to read it for my job.

3 Work in groups. Use some of the language from Exercise 2 to discuss these questions.
   • What languages have you studied?
   • What languages do you know at least a few words in? What can you say?
   • How did you learn? Do you use these languages now? How well do you know each one?

READING

4 You are going to read an article about 'hyperglots' – people who speak many languages. Work in pairs. Look at the photos and the title opposite then discuss how these words and numbers might be connected to the topic.

| 72 | a parrot | translator | 10,000 |
| two weeks | globalisation | genes | mistakes |

5 Read the article and check your ideas from Exercise 4.

6 According to the article, are the sentences true (T) or false (F)?
   1 Mezzofanti spoke 72 languages fluently.
   2 Some people who heard Mezzofanti speak probably couldn't know if he was fluent.
   3 There is no proof that Mezzofanti really was multilingual.
   4 Globalisation will create more hyperglots.
   5 Hyperglots often possess genetic advantages.
   6 Hyperglots aim to speak all their languages fluently.

7 Work in pairs. Read the comments that follow the article and discuss these questions.
   • Which comments do you agree with and which do you disagree with? Why?
   • What did you find most interesting about the article?
   • Did you read anything about the habits of hyperglots that could help you study better?

Understanding reading texts and improving your vocabulary involves more than just learning single words. You also need to notice the connected words and grammar.

8 Find these words in the article and notice the connected words and grammar.

| far | evidence | growing |
| allow | terms | opportunities |

9 Work in groups. Cover the article and complete the sentences. Then check your ideas.
   1 But _____ **far** _____ ?
   2 There _____ **evidence** _____ he could use many languages.
   3 There will _____ **growing** _____ in the future.
   4 Top _____ may _____ genes _____ **allow** _____ get the _____ their training.
   5 They often _____ limited _____ **terms** _____ individual languages.
   6 They _____ **opportunities** _____ language closer to home.

10 Work in pairs. Discuss the questions.
   • Think of two examples where there are growing numbers of something. Why are they growing?
   • How is your English in terms of vocabulary, speaking, listening, etc.? What can you do to improve these different aspects?
   • What opportunities do you have to practise English?

HOME | ARTICLES | LANGUAGES | ABOUT | CONTACT

THE GOOGLE TRANSLATORS IN HUMAN FORM

Michael Erard's new book investigates the master linguists or 'hyperglots'

Liam Scanlon

The 18th century Italian priest Cardinal Giuseppe Mezzofanti is a legend among linguists. They say he studied 72 languages, 30 of which he mastered. He spoke another nine fluently, though not perfectly, and could hold a basic conversation in at least eleven more. And all that without leaving Italy! One story suggests he picked up Ukrainian in just two weeks, after meeting a visitor from there.

But how **far** is this true? Certainly, the figure of 72 is too high and some people perhaps exaggerated how fluent he was. He lived at a time when travel was difficult and learning other languages was still unusual. Therefore, many reports of his abilities come from visitors who were probably struggling to express themselves in Italian. There were also those who, while appreciating his good accent and accurate grammar, described him as merely a parrot who said nothing of interest. However, according to Michael Erard, author of the book *Mezzofanti's Gift*, there is sufficient **evidence** to believe he could use many languages.

Erard also argues that there are many hyperglots in the world today and that, with globalisation, there will be a **growing** number in the future. For example, Alexander Arguelles is fluent in around twenty languages and has studied 60. He studies nine hours a day, down from fourteen before he got married! The Hungarian translator Kato Lomb worked with sixteen, and you can watch a YouTube video of Alex Rawling speaking eleven languages at the age of twenty.

A central question of the book is whether hyperglots are born or made. Are their achievements genetic or do hyperglots have secrets that normal language learners can learn from? Erard's conclusions agree with research on highly talented people in other areas such as sport and music. These people generally have advantages they are born with: top athletes may have genes that **allow** them to get the most from their training; hyperglots seem to possess excellent memories and have brains that are more efficient in processing speech sounds. However, becoming the best also requires a lot of hard work. Some argue that the difference between a top performer and someone who's just 'very good' is that the top performer has practised for 10,000 hours instead of 6,000.

The fact is that most ordinary language learners lack these natural advantages and simply don't have that much time. So is there any hope for us? Erard believes there is and that research on hyperglots can offer some useful lessons. For example, they often have limited ambitions in **terms** of individual languages: they're happy to get by, or to be only able to read, or not to have a perfect accent. They're practical: if they can't travel, they look for **opportunities** to use the language closer to home. Some simply imagine conversations in their heads. They also use other techniques like learning words in context. Finally, they're never afraid to make mistakes or appear stupid and so never give up.

Cardinal Giuseppe Mezzofanti

COMMENTS

langlearner: I've actually read Kato's book about language learning and I think the best advice is to read what you're interested in and read a lot.

bobjob: I know it's wrong, but I kind of hate these people! I'm struggling to learn one extra language.

unconvinced: How does Alexander Arguelles earn a living? I think you need to be rich to be a hyperglot!

hughd: You have to start learning languages when you're young.

andyw: When people say they're bad at languages, they just mean they don't want to spend the time required to learn.

artist: I can say 'do you work or study' in fifteen languages. Does that make me a hyperglot?

r_sewell: The thing about vocabulary in context is good. I never learn single words. I always learn words in groups.

Unit 1 First class

PUTTING YOUR WORDS TO WORK

SPEAKING

1 Work in pairs. Discuss the questions.
   - Where and when do you use English outside the classroom?
   - What do you do most: read, listen, speak or write?
   - When was the first time you used English outside a classroom? What did you talk about? How successful was it?
   - What's been your best moment using English outside the classroom? Why was it good?

LISTENING

2 ▶5 Listen to three people telling stories connected to speaking a foreign language. Match two sentences to each speaker (1–3). There are two sentences you do not need.
   a They helped someone by using a foreign language.
   b Their parents fell in love in Rio de Janeiro.
   c They have an unusual family background.
   d They were involved in a misunderstanding.
   e Their parents speak together in a foreign language.
   f They filmed an animal attacking someone.
   g They changed their behaviour as a result of the experience.
   h They work with people from other countries.

3 ▶5 Listen again and complete the sentences with three words in each space. Contractions count as one word.
   1 a Two Chinese guys _____ me and stopped me.
     b They started talking really fast, you know, and I _____ at all!
     c I asked them to slow down, and then, _____ of my bad Chinese and gesture, I explained …
   2 a He worked in the engine room and she was _____ .
     b My mum said Dad was a really good dancer, _____ very difficult to believe.
     c They also said it _____ about whose country to live in.
   3 a We go all over the place _____ unusual wild animals.
     b We often need _____ local people to act as guides or cooks for the film crew.
     c Anyway, last year we were filming in Sumatra in _____ a forest …

4 Work in groups. Discuss the questions.
   - Which of the stories did you like the best? Why?
   - Do you know any families where they speak more than one language? Why?
   - Have you ever been on a cruise? When? Where?
   - Have you ever helped anyone in the street? Where? What did you do?
   - Do you know any 'false friends' – words that look or sound the same, but have a different meaning in different languages?

GRAMMAR Narrative tenses

5 Look at these sentences from the stories. Then complete the rules below.
   a *They first **looked** really surprised and then they **started** talking really fast, you know.*
   b *It was actually the first time I**'d spoken** to anyone Chinese outside of my class.*
   c *They first **met** when they **were** both **working** on a cruise ship.*
   d *Neither **spoke** each other's language, but my mum **had worked** in Germany before.*
   e *Last year we **were filming** in the middle of a forest … and one time at dinner I **was talking** to the guide and I **tried** to ask about 'the people of the inner forest' …*

We use three main tenses when telling stories: the past simple, the past continuous and the past perfect simple.
- Past simple: add _____ to the infinitive (without *to*) of the verb. Some past forms are irregular, e.g. _____ .
- Past continuous: use _____ / _____ + *-ing* form of the verb.
- Past perfect simple: use _____ + past participle. Some participles are irregular, e.g. _____ .

---

6 Look at the sentences in Exercise 5 again and answer the questions.
   1 Which tense is the most common in telling stories?
   2 Which tense is often used at the beginning of the story to give background information?
   3 Which tense shows the events followed each other in order?
   4 Which tense shows the 'past in the past' – an action that happened before something else we talked about?
   5 Which tense shows an action was unfinished or stopped by another action?

G Check your ideas on page 86 and do Exercise 1.

7 Read this story about how another person's parents met. Decide if the past simple forms are correct or not. Correct the ones which are wrong.

I love the story of how my parents met. My dad was twenty. One day my dad ¹*taked* an overnight train to Prague in Czech Republic and during the night he ²*fell* asleep. When he ³*waked* up, he realised they ⁴*was* in Prague so he rushed to get off the train. He ⁵*see* a policeman looking at someone's papers and he suddenly realised he ⁶*hadn't* his passport or money or phone. He ⁷*ran* back to the train. He sat down, but then this guy ⁸*came* up to him and asked him something in Czech. He then said in English, 'What's the matter?' and so my dad ⁹*explained*. So basically, this guy, who was called Anton, ¹⁰*helped* him. He took my dad home, ¹¹*given* him something to eat, ¹²*let* him phone his parents to get some money – everything. And later that evening my dad met Anton's parents … and he met his sister. And that's how he met my mother!

PRONUNCIATION

8 ▶6 Some of the details of the story in Exercise 7 are missing. Listen and write down the eight phrases and sentences you hear. You will hear each twice: first fast and then slower.

9 ▶7 Listen again to the faster version. Notice the weak forms of the auxiliaries: *was* /wəz/, *were* /wə/, *had* /əd/. Practise saying the phrases and sentences as quickly as you can.

10 Work in pairs. Decide where each of the eight phrases and sentences from Exercise 8 should go in the story in Exercise 7.

11 Complete the sentences with your own ideas.
   1 When I got home, I suddenly realised …
   2 I didn't recognise her at first because …
   3 I wasn't looking where I was going and …
   4 This guy came up to me and …
   5 I had meant to say … , but I'd actually said …
   6 I found out later that …

12 Work in pairs. Compare your ideas from Exercise 11 and decide which is the most interesting. Then write a story around the sentence.

G For further practice, see Exercise 2 on page 87.

SPEAKING

13 Choose two of these ideas for stories. Spend a few minutes thinking about what happened and how you will tell the stories.
   - the first time your parents met
   - the first time you met your best friend / wife / husband / boyfriend / girlfriend
   - a time when you forgot or lost something important
   - a time you had a good or funny experience using a foreign language
   - a time a stranger helped you or you helped a stranger

14 Work in groups. Share your stories.

Unit 1 First class 13

2

FEELINGS

IN THIS UNIT YOU LEARN HOW TO:

- talk about how you feel – and why
- respond to good and bad news
- talk about your life now
- explain why you can't – or don't want to – do things

SPEAKING

1 **Work in pairs. Discuss the questions.**
   - Who do you think the people are?
   - How do you think each person is feeling? Why?
   - What happened before the picture was taken?
   - How does the picture make you feel?

2 **Work with a new partner. Tell each other about the last time you felt:**
   - very happy.
   - very tired.
   - quite annoyed.

3 **What other words do you know to describe feelings?**

Unit 2 Feelings 15

ARE YOU OK?

VOCABULARY Feelings

1 Match the words in bold in the sentences to these basic meanings: *happy, annoyed, tired, bad, sad, angry, worried*.
   1 We left at six in the morning and didn't get back till midnight. I was **exhausted**.
   2 You must be really **pleased** with the results. They're great.
   3 She was absolutely **furious** when she saw the mess that they had made.
   4 I'm under so much pressure at work. I'm really **stressed** about everything.
   5 His dog died last night. He was very **upset** when I spoke to him. He sounded as if he might cry.
   6 I'm so sorry. I feel really **guilty** about leaving you with all the work to do.
   7 Ask her now. She looks like she's **in a good mood**. She might say yes.
   8 It was good to see her happy and enjoying herself because I know she's been a bit **down**.
   9 I was **pleasantly surprised** by the film. I really didn't expect it to be so good.
   10 I'm **fed up** with this weather. It's so hot you can't do anything. I've had enough of it!

2 Work in pairs. Answer the questions.
   1 Can you find the five prepositions connected to adjectives in Exercise 1?
   2 Why else might you feel exhausted?
   3 How do you know if someone is pleased with something?
   4 How do you know when someone is furious?
   5 Why might someone get upset?
   6 What other things might you feel guilty / bad about?
   7 What things might put you in a good mood?
   8 What's the opposite of being pleasantly surprised?

LISTENING

3 ▶ 8 Listen to two conversations. The first is between two people talking about their friend Karim. The second is between two women, Belinda and Alisha. How do these three people feel?
   1 Karim   2 Belinda   3 Alisha

4 ▶ 8 Do you remember why they feel this way? Listen again and check your ideas.

5 Work in pairs. Discuss the questions.
   • What would you do or say if a friend was upset? Would it be different if it was a man or a woman?
   • What kind of things do you do to cheer yourself up if you are a bit down?
   • Are you good at sorting out problems?
   • Who do you talk to if you have a problem?

GRAMMAR

Linking verbs

Be, look, seem, feel, sound, taste and *smell* are all linking verbs. These verbs can be followed by different patterns.

6 Look at these sentences from Exercise 1 and the conversations. Then work in pairs and answer the questions below.
   a That chocolate cake **looks** nice.
   b He **seemed** a bit down.
   c He **sounded** as if he might cry.
   d She **looks** like she's in a good mood.
   e That **sounds** like a nightmare.

   1 What is the pattern when an adjective comes after a linking verb?
   2 What two patterns are possible when a clause comes after a linking verb?
   3 What is the pattern when a noun comes after a linking verb?

G Check your ideas on page 87 and do Exercise 1.

7 Complete the sentences with the correct form of the verbs. You may also need to add other words.
   1 Are you OK? You _____ a bit stressed. (look)
   2 Are you all right? You _____ you've seen a ghost. (look)
   3 Is Julie OK? She _____ disappointed when I spoke to her. (sound)
   4 Is Mike all right? He _____ a bit down. (seem)

16

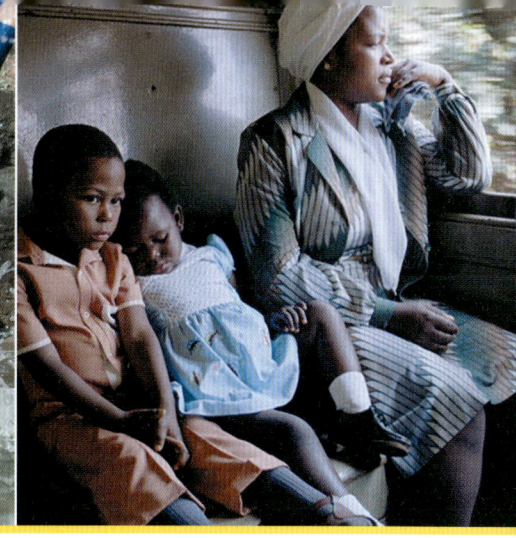

5 Are you OK? You _____ you've got a cold. (sound)
6 Are you all right? You _____ a bit confused. (look)
7 Have you seen Ana? She _____ so well, so relaxed when I saw her last! (look)
8 Hi. You _____ you're in a very good mood. (look)

8 Match 1–8 from Exercise 7 with the responses (a–h).

a Yeah, I've just found out I've got a new job. I'm really pleased.
b Yeah, I know. She's so much better after that holiday.
c Yeah, I feel terrible. I think I've maybe got flu.
d I am. I'm really behind with work and I'm exhausted.
e Yeah, I don't understand this. What am I supposed to do?
f Yeah. Well, on my way here I was almost hit by this guy who was driving like an idiot.
g He's just split up with Jo and he's quite upset about it.
h Yeah. I think she expected to get a better mark as she'd studied so much.

9 Write your own responses to 1–8 in Exercise 7. Then work in pairs. Take turns reading out 1–8 and giving your own responses.

DEVELOPING CONVERSATIONS

Response expressions

We use lots of short expressions to respond to news. Look at these examples from the conversations. Notice how we often ask a question after the response.

C: *Apparently, she's quite ill and he's just very worried about her.*
R: **Oh no!** *That sounds like a nightmare. What's wrong with her? Is it very serious?*

B: *I've just found out I can't continue to stay where I am at the moment.*
A: **What a pain!** *How come?*

10 Complete the exchanges with these words.

| Congratulations | Oh no | a shame |
| a relief | Wow | a pain |

1 A: I can't drink at the moment. I'm pregnant.
  B: Really? _____ ! When is the baby due?
2 A: I'm going to Canada to study English.
  B: _____ ! That's great! How long are you going for?
3 A: I'm afraid I can't meet you tonight.
  B: Oh, what _____ ! Are you sure?
4 A: My brother's not very well.
  B: _____ ! I'm really sorry. I hope it's not too serious.
5 A: I've lost my wallet.
  B: Oh no! What _____ ! Did it have much in it?
6 A: I've found my wallet!
  B: Phew, that's _____ ! Where was it?

PRONUNCIATION

11 ▶ 9 Listen and check your answers to Exercise 10. Notice how the intonation changes when responding to good and bad news. Then work in pairs and practise the exchanges.

CONVERSATION PRACTICE

12 Work in pairs. Each think of a piece of good or bad news. Write a conversation like the ones you heard in Exercise 3. Include response expressions.

13 Try to remember your conversation. Act it out in front of another pair of students.

2 To watch the video and do the activities, see the DVD ROM.

Unit 2 Feelings 17

HUGS AND KISSES

SPEAKING

1 Check you understand the words and phrases in bold. Then work in groups and discuss the questions.

- How often do you do these things? In what situations?
  - **hug** people
  - **kiss** people **on the cheek** or **lips**
  - walk **arm in arm** with people or **hold hands**
  - **shake hands** or **bow**
  - touch people on the arm or **put** your arm **round their shoulder**
- Do you do any of these things more often or less often than most people in your country? Why?
- Have you been anywhere where they do these things differently to you? Where? What do they do?

READING

2 Work in pairs. Look at the photo opposite and discuss the questions.

- What is the man in the photo doing? Why do you think he's doing this?
- What would you do if you saw someone like this? Why?
- Are there any famous local characters in your local area / town / city? Why are they well known?

3 Read the article. Answer the questions.

1 What made Juan Mann start his campaign?
2 How did he feel when he went out for the first time?
3 Who first asked for a hug, and why?
4 How did Mann become so famous?
5 What two theories are put forward to explain the success of the Free Hugs movement?

4 Work in pairs. Cover the article. Try to remember the adjectives that went with these nouns. Then look at the article and check your answers.

1 _____ connections
2 a _____ attempt
3 an _____ star
4 his _____ identity
5 a _____ year
6 one of the _____ shopping districts
7 _____ skills
8 _____ experiences

LISTENING

5 ▶10 Work in pairs. Discuss what impact success probably had on Juan Mann and what you think happened to his campaign. Then listen and check your ideas.

6 Work in pairs. Discuss the questions.

- Do you think Juan Mann was right to walk away from the Free Hugs 'brand'? Why? / Why not?
- Why do think the Free Hugs movement has been controversial in some countries?
- Do you think it has a future? Would it be popular in your country? Why? / Why not?

UNDERSTANDING VOCABULARY

-ed / -ing adjectives

A small group of common adjectives can end in both *-ed* and *-ing*. The *-ed* form describes people's feelings. The *-ing* form describes the things that cause the feelings.

In the modern world, it is not unusual for **people** to feel **depressed**.

It was a **depressing time**.

7 Complete the pairs of sentences with the correct adjective form of these verbs.

| annoy | confuse | bore |
| depress | shock | disappoint |

1 a Can you explain it again? I'm still a bit _____ .
  b The instructions for this camera are really _____ .
2 a He has a really _____ habit of repeating the same stories over and over again.
  b I'm a bit _____ that he hasn't phoned me. He promised to!
3 a He's been _____ for a while, but he refuses to try counselling.
  b This weather's so _____ . It's so cold and wet!
4 a I found the violence in the film quite _____ , to be honest.
  b I was really _____ to see so many homeless people on the streets there!
5 a I'm _____ . Can't we go out somewhere?
  b I find her quite _____ . All she ever talks about is her children!
6 a Obviously, I'm a bit _____ that I didn't get the job.
  b I loved her last film, but to be honest I found this one quite _____ .

8 Complete the sentences so they are true for you.

1 I find it really annoying when people …
2 The last time I got really bored was when …
3 I always get really depressed when …
4 One thing I found really disappointing was …
5 The most shocking thing I've ever seen was …
6 I still get quite confused about …

9 Work in groups. Compare your sentences and explain your ideas. Who do you have most in common with?

IT ONLY TAKES JUAN MANN TO CHANGE THE WORLD!

In the modern world, it is not unusual for people to feel depressed or isolated. It can be hard to make **meaningful connections** with others. That was certainly how the mysterious Juan Mann ('One man') felt – until the day he decided to start giving free hugs to strangers. What started as a **desperate attempt** to change his own life subsequently transformed him into an **international star**.

On returning to Sydney, Australia, in early 2004, after travelling in Europe, Mann (who has always kept his **true identity** secret) had a **miserable year**. His parents had divorced and he found himself lonely and unemployed. It was a depressing time as many of his friends were no longer around and his family was also elsewhere. After spending months hiding away from the world, feeling sad and sorry for himself, he decided to change his life and do something completely different.

And something different is exactly what he did! Mann went to one of Sydney's **main shopping districts** holding a cardboard sign saying 'Free Hugs' – and waited. He expected to last an hour at the most and had even asked a friend to come along to protect him. He also very deliberately left his wallet at home.

After fifteen minutes, however, a woman approached him and said that her dog had died that morning and on top of that it was the first anniversary of her daughter's death, so she could really use a hug. Mann was happy to help!

His 'Free Hugs' campaign continued quietly for a couple of years until a songwriter he knew filmed him in action. This friend then added a song by his own band Sick Puppies and posted the video on YouTube, where it has now had over 75 million hits. Mann quickly became something of a celebrity, was interviewed by legendary American chat show host Oprah Winfrey and saw Free Hugs go global, with similar groups appearing all over the world.

Mann seemed to find the success of his project funny as he had been told at school that he lacked the **social skills** to work with people in need, yet had ended up as a kind of therapist for a whole city. His explanation was that many people needed someone to listen to their problems, but were too embarrassed to call a helpline or seek counselling.

To some, the growth of the Free Hugs movement is a sign that acts of kindness are becoming more socially acceptable. In an age when nobody expects to get something for nothing and where economic competition and greed have become the norm, perhaps the movement offers a different, softer approach to life. Also, **shared experiences** in the real world may be more important to us now that we spend so much time in virtual online worlds.

However, the most incredible aspect of Juan Mann's story has not been the effect it has had on those he shared hugs with or even on those inspired by his story, but actually the effect it has had on himself.

IT'S SO GOOD TO SEE YOU!

SPEAKING

bump into /ˌbʌmp ˈɪntə/ (phrasal verb)
If you bump into someone you know, you unexpectedly meet them somewhere – when you have not planned to.

1 Work in pairs. Discuss the questions.
   - Where you live, in what places do you often bump into people you know?
   - What's the most surprising time you've bumped into someone? Why was it so unexpected?
   - When was the last time you bumped into someone? Where was it? What did you talk about?
   - Is there a famous person you would like to bump into? What would you ask them?
   - Is there anyone you wouldn't want to bump into? Why?

LISTENING

2 ▶11 Listen to two people, Carla and Robin, who bump into each other in the street. Are the sentences true (T), false (F) or not mentioned (N)?
   1 Carla and Robin went to school together.
   2 Robin has put on a lot of weight since they last met.
   3 Carla isn't working today.
   4 Carla is a website designer.
   5 Her work is very busy at the moment.
   6 Carla lives with her boyfriend.
   7 Robin has a part-time job at the moment.
   8 Robin's parents are separated.
   9 Carla is really into running.
   10 Robin would like to run a marathon.

3 ▶11 Listen again and complete the sentences with two words in each space. Contractions count as one word.
   1 Sorry. I just _____ you. You look so different.
   2 I do sales _____ for a film company.
   3 That's amazing. I'm really _____ you.
   4 I'm working really _____ .
   5 I'm learning a lot and the money's not bad either, so I _____ .
   6 OK. And are you still living _____ ?
   7 She still talks about you from time _____ .
   8 That's my idea _____ !

4 Work in pairs. Discuss the questions.
   - Have you ever failed to recognise someone you knew? Why?
   - Would you like to work in sales and marketing? Why? / Why not?
   - Do you know anyone who's getting married sometime soon?
   - Do you know anyone who is out of work at the moment?
   - Do you know anyone who trains regularly? What for?
   - What's your idea of hell?

GRAMMAR

Present simple and present continuous

The present simple uses the infinitive form of the verb (without *to*). The third person form adds an *-s*.

I **work** in sales and marketing.

The present continuous uses a form of the auxiliary verb *be* and the *-ing* form of the verb.

We**'re setting** up a new website at the moment.

5 Look at these sentences from the conversation. Answer the questions below.
   a We**'re getting** married in the summer.
   b She**'s staying** with her brother on the coast.
   c I **train** on Saturdays.

   1 Which sentence is about a habit or a regular repeated activity?
   2 Which sentence is about a temporary, unfinished activity?
   3 Which sentence is about something in the future that is already arranged with other people?
   4 Do you know what the connection is between these verbs?

   | agree | believe | belong | disagree | forget |
   | like | need | own | seem | want |

G Check your ideas on page 87 and do Exercise 1.

20

6 Put the words in italics into either the present simple or the present continuous. Use contractions where possible.

1. A: How *your course / go*? Are you still enjoying it?
   B: Yeah, although *I / find* / it a lot harder than before.
2. A: Are you busy this weekend? *you / want / go out* / somewhere?
   B: *I / work* / Saturday mornings, but I'm free in the afternoon.
3. A: What's your sister doing these days? *she / still / study*?
   B: Yeah. She graduated last year, but now *she / do* / a Master's.
4. A: *I / need* / a coat? Is it still raining outside?
   B: Yeah, *it / pour* / down.
5. A: *you / have* / any plans for tonight?
   B: Yeah. *I / meet* / an old friend of mine for dinner, actually.
6. A: What's the matter with him? Why *he / shout* / at everyone like that?
   B: I don't know. He's just in a bad mood. *he / get* / like this sometimes.

PRONUNCIATION

7 ▶12 Listen to the present continuous sentences in Exercise 6 – first said slowly and then faster. Notice the contractions and the weak forms of the verb *be*.

8 Work in pairs. Practise reading out the exchanges in Exercise 6. How quickly can you say them?

If you say you can't or don't want to do something, it's polite to give a reason. The reason will often use the present simple or present continuous. Look at this extract from the conversation:

R: *What are you doing this Saturday? Do you want to meet for lunch or something?*
C: *Oh, I'd love to, but I* **train** *on Saturdays. I'm doing the marathon next month.*

---

9 Write reasons to explain why you can't or don't want to do the things below. Use the present simple or present continuous.

1. A: Do you think you could help me move this table?
   B: No, sorry but I can't. _____
2. A: We're going out for dinner later. Would you like to join us?
   B: Oh, I'd love to, but I can't. _____
3. A: Can I just use your computer for a few minutes?
   B: No, sorry. _____
4. A: Can you turn this music off? It's driving me mad.
   B: No, leave it on. _____
5. A: Would you like to go out with me on Friday?
   B: Oh, it's nice of you to ask, but I can't. Sorry. _____

10 Work in pairs. Take turns reading out the questions in Exercise 9. Say your responses and continue each conversation for as long as you can.

G For further practice, see Exercise 2 on page 88.

SPEAKING

11 Work in pairs. You are going to roleplay a conversation between two old friends who bump into each other in the street.

Student A: read File 3 on page 98.

Student B: read File 7 on page 99.

12 Now roleplay the conversation. Use some of the language below.

- I haven't seen you for ages.
- How have you been?
- It's so good to see you.
- So what are you doing here?
- So what are doing these days?
- How's your family?
- Anyway, listen. I'm actually in a bit of a rush.
- We must meet again sometime.

Unit 2 Feelings 21

VIDEO 1

KENYA COMES TO CENTRAL PARK

1 Work in pairs. Look at the photo and imagine you met these people.
   - What might you say to them? What questions would you ask?
   - What things do you think you might have in common with them?

2 **▶ 3** Watch the first part of a video about two men like those in the photo (0.00–1.28). Find out:
   1 why they are running in the park.
   2 where they are from.
   3 what they have in common with the man they talk to.

3 The words and phrases below all appear in the second part of the video. Work in pairs. Check you understand them, then discuss what you think might happen in the second part of the video.

1 East Africa	5 leopards
2 The Bronx	6 sticks
3 some issues	7 elephant dung
4 sheets and blankets	8 the rest of my life

4 **▶ 3** Watch the second part of the video where the two men meet someone called Jimmy (1.29–4.51). Find out why the words and phrases in Exercise 3 are used. Then compare your ideas with your partner.

5 Work in groups. Discuss the questions.
   - What do you think of what happens in the video?
   - Why do you think Jimmy sleeps in the park?
   - Would you find it easy to start conversations like this in a park? Why? / Why not?
   - Have you ever made a fire? Where? How?
   - How well would you survive living outside? Why?
   - Tell your group about one experience that will stay with you for the rest of your life.

UNDERSTANDING FAST SPEECH

6 **▶ 4** Read and listen to this extract from the video said at natural pace and then slowed down. To help you, groups of words are marked with / and pauses are marked //. Stressed sounds are in CAPITALS.

You know YEAH / we GOTta hang OUT someTIME / you KNOW // You KNOW you VISit HERE / any time you HERE you VISit US / and any TIME we're over THERE / we COME VISit YOU

7 Now you have a go! Practise saying the extract at natural pace.

REVIEW 1

GRAMMAR

1 Complete the text with one word in each space. Contractions count as one word.

Have I ever told you how my parents met? I don't think I ¹_____ . Well, they met in the middle of nowhere in Peru. My dad ²_____ walking on his own to the lost city of Machu Picchu. He was very fit at the time, but found he was ³_____ slower and slower and then he stopped and was really sick. Apparently, it ⁴_____ caused by being so high up in the mountains. Eventually, he got to a little village to ask for help, which was a bit difficult as he ⁵_____ speak much Spanish. Fortunately, there was another group who ⁶_____ just visited Machu Picchu and were on their way back to the nearest city, Cuzco. My mum was in that group. She had ⁷_____ Spanish at university, so she translated for him. She told me that ⁸_____ she first saw him, she was really shocked because he looked ⁹_____ if he was dying! Fortunately, he ¹⁰_____ ! My dad recovered and they fell in love. And that's why they ¹¹_____ going back to Machu Picchu later this year to celebrate their 25th wedding anniversary. My dad still ¹²_____ been there!

2 Make two questions from each group of words (1–6).

1 Where / What / does / are / that / you / based / involve
2 Have / Are / you / you / working / been / here before / at the moment
3 Where / When / does / was / she / she / live / born
4 Did / Has / you / she / go out / seen / it / last night
5 What / How / kind of music / often / do / are / you / you / into / do that
6 How many / How long / have / brothers and sisters / do / you / you / been / have / doing that

3 Choose the correct option.

1 What do you do when *you're not* / *you don't* working?
2 Are you OK? You *look* / *look like* a bit confused.
3 Sorry, I can't speak to you now. *I do* / *I'm doing* something.
4 Why don't you come round on Friday? We *have* / *are having* a barbecue for my birthday.
5 We couldn't get back into the house because I *left* / *had left* my key inside.
6 Is Hasan OK? He *sounded* / *sounded like* he was getting a cold.
7 It was stupid. I *was trying* / *had tried* to carry too many things and in the end I dropped everything.
8 I asked them to turn their music down because I *was studying* / *studied*.
9 He said he can't come on Friday because he *has* / *is having* too much work.
10 We *met* / *were meeting* some clients when we *heard* / *was hearing* the news.

4 ▶ 13 Listen and write the six sentences you hear.

5 Write a sentence before and after the sentences from Exercise 4 to create short dialogues.

VOCABULARY

6 Match the verbs (1–8) with the collocates (a–h).

1 express   a hands / her head
2 shake   b myself understood / a mess
3 pick it up   c frustrated / the most from the class
4 hold   d myself clearly / his feelings
5 get   e as you go along / slowly
6 make   f hands / a conversation
7 find it   g the language / the basics first
8 master   h difficult to believe / annoying

7 Decide if these words and phrases are connected to relationships, language or feelings.

accent	fluent	mood	get by
only child	furious	accurate	twin
down	single	separated	upset

8 Complete the sentences. Use the word in brackets to form a word that fits in the space.

1 I didn't expect it to be very good, so I was _____ surprised. (pleasant)
2 I struggled with German at school because I just found the grammar so _____ . (confuse)
3 We were quite _____ with the results of the research. (disappoint)
4 Did you see the news yesterday? It was quite _____ , wasn't it? (shock)
5 I think it's easier to remember words if you can make a meaningful _____ to your own language. (connect)
6 Apparently, he can speak six languages _____ . (fluent)
7 Meeting her again after all these years, I had a _____ of emotions. (mix)
8 My flight was overnight and I didn't sleep at all, so I'm _____ . (exhaust)

9 Complete the extract from an email with one word in each space. The first letters are given.

By the way, did I tell you I ¹bu_____ into Brian in town the other day? It was a bit ²em_____ actually because I didn't ³re_____ him at first as he's grown this huge beard. I was walking along and this guy came ⁴u_____ t_____ me and he looked as if he was about to hit me and I actually screamed. Then he said his name and of course I just laughed with ⁵re_____ and I gave him a big ⁶h_____ . We were in the ⁷mi_____ of the supermarket so we got quite a few strange looks. He's actually doing really well. You know he was working as a civil ⁸s_____ ? Well he left that job last year and he's gone back to university. He's studying ⁹Me_____ . His brother was ill for a while and Brian did some ¹⁰re_____ into his illness as a way to support him and now he wants to do more. I think he was also a bit ¹¹f_____ u_____ of his old job and he'll have far more ¹²op_____ when he gets his degree. It really was great to see him.

Review 1   23

3

IN THIS UNIT YOU LEARN HOW TO:

- describe places and explain where they are
- give and respond to suggestions
- discuss future plans
- talk about the weather
- recognise and reuse useful chunks of language
- ask and talk about holiday experiences

SPEAKING

1 Work in groups. Look at the photo and discuss the questions.

- Would you like to go to a place like this for a holiday? Why? / Why not?
- What's the best place to get a view where you live? What can you see from there?
- What's the highest building or place you have been up? How was it? When did you go there?

TIME OFF

CAN YOU RECOMMEND ANYWHERE?

VOCABULARY Places of interest

1 Complete the sentences with these words. Then check you understand the words and phrases in bold.

| gallery | ruins | walls | old town | lake |
| nightlife | palace | mosque | stalls | theme park |

1 There's a _____ about a mile out of town, where you can **hire a boat** and **go fishing**.
2 There's an old **castle** above the city. You can walk along the _____ and go to the top of the **tower**.
3 There's a **street market** in the east of the city with _____ selling everything from **antiques** to apples.
4 There's an old **royal** _____ down by the river. It reopened recently **after being restored**.
5 There's a really fun _____ further along the coast. They've got some **great rides** there.
6 The main _____ is in the old Jewish **district**. There are lots of bars and restaurants there and it's always very **lively**.
7 There are Roman _____ all over this part of the country. They **discovered** some near here recently.
8 There's a beautiful _____ near here. You'll hear the **call to prayer** in the morning.
9 They built a new **modern art** _____ recently. It's an amazing building. It was **designed** by a famous Brazilian **architect**.
10 Most of the _____ was built in **the 17th century**, but there's a famous church which is **medieval**.

2 Work in pairs. Think of a word or phrase connected to each of the words in the box in Exercise 1. Use a dictionary to help you.

gallery – exhibition   lake – go for a swim

3 Complete the phrases with prepositions from Exercise 1.
1 It's about ten miles / sixty kilometres / an hour _____ of town.
2 You can walk _____ the walls / the river / the beach.
3 It's _____ the east of the city / the financial district / the old town.
4 It's _____ by the river / the beach / the lake.
5 It's further _____ the coast / the river / the canal.
6 You find them all _____ this part of the country / this area / the city.

PRONUNCIATION

4 ▶14 Listen to some of the phrases in Exercise 3 said slowly. Notice how consonant sounds link to vowel sounds.

5 ▶14 Listen again and practise saying the phrases in the same slow way. Then practise saying them as quickly as you can.

6 Think of a tourist destination you know well. Spend a few minutes preparing a short presentation about the place and what you can see and do there. Try to use some of the vocabulary from Exercises 1–3. Then work in groups and give your presentations to each other.

LISTENING

7 Look at the places to visit in and around Kraków, Poland's top tourist destination. Work in pairs. Decide which places you would go to and why.

KRAKÓW
PLACES TO VISIT

RYNEK GŁÓWNY
A huge medieval square in the centre of the old town where there is a market with some great stalls.

ULICA JÓZEFA
This street is full of shops selling products by Poland's top designers.

MOCAK
Kraków's modern art gallery, designed by the Italian architect Claudio Nardi.

ST. MARY'S CHURCH
The city's most important church, built in the sixteenth century.

KAZIMIERZ
The old Jewish district, now a lively area with excellent nightlife.

NOWA HUTA
The industrial and housing district built in the 1950s during the communist time.

CIEN
The best club in town. Tues–Sat from 10 till the last guest leaves.

NEAR KRAKÓW
Half-day tour to Wieliczka Salt Mine. Go down and see the amazing underground world of these ancient mines.

FULL-DAY TOUR TO THE TATRAS MOUNTAINS
Enjoy a day's walking in this beautiful location.

FULL-DAY TOUR TO AUSCHWITZ-BIRKENAU MUSEUM
Auschwitz-Birkenau was a Nazi concentration camp during World War II.

8 ▶15 Listen to a conversation between a tourist and a hotel receptionist in Kraków. Which of the places in Kraków are mentioned? What does the tourist decide to do? Work in pairs and compare your ideas.

9 ▶15 Complete the sentences with one word in each space. Then listen again and check your answers.

1 Hello there. I _____ if you can help me.
2 I'm _____ of going sightseeing today.
3 Can you _____ anywhere good to go?
4 It depends on _____ you like.
5 I'm not really a big _____ of churches, to be honest.
6 Well, in that case, you _____ try Kazimierz.
7 How _____ a guided tour of Nowa Huta?
8 I can call and _____ a _____ for you, if you want.

DEVELOPING CONVERSATIONS
Giving and responding to suggestions

10 Put the two conversations into the correct order. The first one is done for you.

Conversation 1

a **Well, you could try** Oxford Street. There are lots of big department stores there.
b Oh, OK. Well, **in that case, how about** Portobello Road? It's a big street market. You can find lots of bargains there.
c **To be honest, I'm not really a big fan of** department stores.
d **Oh, that sounds great. I love that kind of thing.** Is it easy to get to?
e **I'm thinking of** doing some shopping today. **Can you recommend anywhere?**   1
f Yes, very. I'll show you on the map.

Conversation 2

g Right. **I'm not really into** museums, to be honest.
h Well, you could try the local museum. That's quite close to here. They've got lots of interesting things in there.
i No, it's quite cheap. It should only be about $10.
j I'm thinking of doing some sightseeing today. Can you recommend anywhere?
k Oh, **that sounds better**. Are they expensive to get into?
l That's OK. In that case, **how about going to** the Roman ruins down by the lake? There are also some nice cafés and you can swim there.

11 ▶16 Listen and check your answers. Then work in pairs and practise reading the conversations.

CONVERSATION PRACTICE

12 Make a list of places in your town / area that you think are good for visitors to go to.

13 Work in pairs. You are going to roleplay a conversation between a tourist and a hotel receptionist in the place where you live.

Student A: you are the tourist. You are thinking of going sightseeing. Ask for recommendations. Reject some before deciding on one.

Student B: you are the hotel receptionist. Suggest some different places to the tourist. Explain why they are good.

14 Now roleplay the conversation. Try to use some of the phrases in bold from Exercise 10. When you have finished, change roles and have another conversation.

5 To watch the video and do the activities, see the DVD ROM.

KRAKÓW
PLACES TO VISIT

Unit 3 Time off 27

MY KIND OF HOLIDAY

LISTENING

1 Work in pairs. Look at the photos and the descriptions of people and holidays. What do you know about the places in the photos? Which people do you think go with which holiday? Explain your decisions.

2 ▶ 17 Listen to three people talking about their holiday plans for this year and answer the questions.

 1 Which of the people in the photos are talking?
 2 Where is each person having their holiday?
 3 What other places do they mention?

3 ▶ 17 Decide which of the following things are important for each speaker (1–3) when planning their holiday. There is one you do not need. Then listen again and check your ideas.

 a nice accommodation
 b evening entertainment and nightlife
 c guaranteed good weather
 d sights and history
 e meeting local people
 f mountains or beautiful countryside
 g good food
 h peace and quiet
 i extra activities (e.g. tennis, sailing, diving, climbing)

SPEAKING

4 When choosing a holiday, what is most important for you? Rank the things in Exercise 3 from 1 (= most important) to 9 (= least important). Make some notes to explain why.

5 Work in groups and compare your choices. Who in your group would make the best partners to go on holiday with? Where might you go and what might you do?

WENDY, 45
A British teacher with teenage kids.

WALEED, 19
A Saudi student with parents and sisters.

LIAN, 61
A retired Chinese civil servant with husband.

ALAIN, 27
A French waiter on his own.

Vietnam in November

Florida, USA in August

London, UK in August

Oman in July

GRAMMAR

Future plans

When we talk about plans in the future, we can use a variety of forms: *will*; *be going to*; the present continuous; *have to*; *may / might*; *be thinking of*.

6 Look at these sentences from the listening. Answer the questions below.

a We**'re staying** in a five-star hotel, of course.
b So we**'ll probably hire** a car to do off-road.
c I **have to work** long hours in July and August.
d When the season ends, I **might take** a short holiday.
e I**'m going to travel** round Vietnam later in the year.
f So we**'re thinking of going** to a show or two.

1 Which three sentences show plans that are definite – already decided or arranged?
2 Which three sentences show plans which are less certain?
3 Which sentence shows a plan which is an obligation?
4 Do you know two questions we often use to ask about future plans?
5 What are the negative forms of each of the structures in a–f?

G Check your ideas on page 88 and do Exercise 1.

7 Complete the conversations with one word in each space. Contractions count as one word.

A: ¹_____ you going away in the summer?
B: Probably, but we're ²_____ to leave it till the last minute to book and try to get a cheap package deal to Greece, or somewhere like that. What about you?
A: Nowhere special. We ³_____ probably just go to my parents' in Scotland. I suppose we ⁴_____ possibly go camping along the coast. We'll see how things go.
B: That sounds nice. What's the weather usually like up there at this time of year?

C: Do you have any ⁵_____ for the weekend?
D: Well, I have an exam next week so I ⁶_____ to do some revision, but I'm ⁷_____ a friend on Sunday morning to go to the Mocak gallery. We ⁸_____ go for lunch too. It depends how much work I do on Saturday. Why? What about you?
C: Well, I'm ⁹_____ of maybe going to the cinema on Saturday night and thought you might like to go, but maybe you ¹⁰_____ be too busy.
D: No. I can work during the day, but then I probably ¹¹_____ want to work in the evening. What are you ¹²_____ of seeing?
C: I haven't decided. Let's have a look now and see what's on.

8 Work in pairs. Discuss the questions.

- Are you going away in the summer?
- Do you have any plans for the weekend?
- What are you doing after the class?
- Are you going to do anything for your birthday?
- Are you going to continue studying English after this course?
- What are you going to do after you leave school / graduate?
- Do you have any plans to change jobs?

G For further practice, see Exercise 2 on page 88.

VOCABULARY Weather

When we want to know about weather in the future, we usually ask one of these questions:

What's the forecast for tomorrow / the weekend?
What's the weather going to be like this afternoon / when you're there?

To talk about predictions we're sure of, we use *will* or *be going to*. To show we're less certain, we use *it'll probably* or *it may / might*.

They said ~~it's raining~~ **it'll probably** rain this afternoon but **it might** clear up by this evening.

9 Match the two parts of the sentences.

1 They said it'll be **hot and humid** during the day, and so
2 They said it's going to be **really windy**, so
3 Apparently, it's going to be **really sunny**, so
4 They said it'll be **freezing** and
5 They said it's going to be **boiling hot** all week and
6 Apparently, it's going to **pour down** tomorrow, so
7 They said it'll be generally **quite warm** during the day, but
8 The same as today: **grey and miserable**, but

a it might **drop to minus** 10°.
b on Tuesday it might **reach** 36°. I hate the heat!
c there might possibly be **a storm** this evening.
d we should take down the parasol or it'll blow away.
e I'll probably stay at home and keep out of the rain!
f I might even get a suntan!
g they said it might **clear up** next week!
h it might get a bit **chilly** at night.

10 Work in pairs. Discuss the questions.

- Do you know what the forecast is for tomorrow / the weekend / next week?
- Are there any bad times to visit where you live because of the weather? Why? When is the best time to visit?
- What's the coldest it gets in your country? What's the hottest?
- How many of the different kinds of weather in Exercise 9 have you had in the last year?

Unit 3 Time off 29

A COMPLETE DISASTER

STRANGE WORLD **LUCY CLEGG**

Is disaster tourism such a total disaster?

For most of us, if we describe a holiday as a disaster, it might mean we got robbed, were stuck indoors as it poured with rain outside, or experienced any number of other things that could spoil our two weeks of relaxation. We generally want to avoid these things. So you might be surprised to learn that there are now companies that actually organise 'disaster experiences' for people looking for adventure in their time off. You can travel to look for a storm – the kind that might blow your house down, not just blow your hat off. Or perhaps you might like to visit a war zone? Visas, travel and accommodation can all be arranged and personal protection can be provided at a cost of anything up to $20,000. How about visiting Chernobyl, the nuclear power plant that exploded in 1986? There is even a company that organises a realistic simulation of a plane crash 'including a smoke-filled cabin.' According to their website, this could provide an excellent day out for employees as a company team-building experience, because 'disasters bring people closer together!' Are they serious? Don't we have enough stress at work without having to pretend we're all going to die!

READING

1 Work in groups. Think of:
- four things that could be described as a disaster.
- four things that could spoil a holiday.

Then discuss whether you have experienced or heard of any of the things. Explain what happened in as much detail as you can.

2 Read the first paragraph of an article about disaster tourism above. Answer the questions.
1 What examples of disaster tourism and disaster experiences are given?
2 What does the author seem to think of disaster tourism?
3 What do you think of it? Would you want to try any of the holidays / days out mentioned?

3 Work in pairs. Look at the four photos in this lesson and discuss the questions.
1 Do you know what countries they are in or why they are famous?
2 How might they be connected to disaster tourism?

Then read the rest of the article in File 2 on page 97 and check your ideas.

4 Read the article again. Find:
1 why the website 'Selfies at serious places' is mentioned.
2 two reasons why the author visits places with bloody histories.
3 the aims of the company Political Tours.
4 two benefits of disaster tourism that James Wilcox mentions.
5 how the author ends up feeling about disaster tourism – and why.

5 Work in groups. Discuss the questions.
- Can you think of other places that tourists visit which have a connection to disasters and death? Would you like to visit them?
- What other benefits of disaster tourism might there be?
- Are there any problems with disaster tourism that the author hasn't mentioned?
- Do you think there are times when / places where you shouldn't take photos or selfies? Why?

UNDERSTANDING VOCABULARY

Useful chunks in texts

A chunk is a group of words that often go together. The words may all be next to each other in a sentence, or they may be spread out across a sentence with other words between the different parts of the chunk. Noticing chunks and thinking about how to use them to express your own ideas is important if you want to get better in a language. We often reuse chunks, but change the words around them.

You might be surprised to learn that there are now companies that actually organise 'disaster experiences.'

You might be surprised to learn that there are more pyramids in Mexico than Egypt.

6 Work in pairs and look at the chunks below. How much can you remember about what the writer said using these chunks? Then look at the article and check your ideas.
1 … my initial reaction when I first … was to …
2 I told myself that there's no way …
3 … which commemorates the people who died …
4 … which was completely destroyed by …
5 … looking at … now, I am wondering …
6 … have a lot to offer.
7 … willing to take the risk and …

7 Write your own sentences using the chunks in Exercise 6. Try to make the sentences true.

*My initial reaction when I first saw the mess in the house after the party **was to** scream!*

8 Work in groups. Compare your sentences and explain as much about them as you can. Who has the best example for each chunk?

Selfie at Chernobyl

GRAMMAR Present perfect simple

9 Look at this extract from the article. Answer the questions below.

*I **have been** to the peace park in Hiroshima, which **commemorates** the people who **died** from the first nuclear bomb. I**'ve visited** many castles like the Tower of London where people **were executed**. Last year I **went** to Pompeii, the ancient ruins of a city which **was** completely **destroyed** by a volcano in the first century. While there, I **took** a photo of a 2,000-year-old dead person.*

1 Which verbs are in the present perfect simple?
2 Do you know how to make the present perfect examples into questions and negatives?
3 Which of these statements are true?
   a The present perfect is often used to introduce experiences connected to a present discussion.
   b When we use the present perfect, we make clear the time of the experience.
   c The details of the experience are usually in the past simple.

G Check your ideas on page 89 and do Exercise 1.

10 Read the Grammar box and answer the questions below.

> When someone asks us a present perfect question, we usually give information or opinions about our experiences – or we ask questions. Note that we often answer using tenses other than the present perfect.

1 Why might someone ask this question?
   Have you been to the theme park along the coast?
2 Which of these answers do you think help to develop the conversation? Why?
   a *Yes, I have.*
   b *Yeah. It's great.*
   c *No, I haven't. Why?*
   d *No.*
   e *Yeah, I went there last year.*

11 Complete these answers to the question *Have you (ever) been to X?* with *Yes* or *No (never)*.

1 _____ . What's it like?
2 _____ , but it's supposed to be amazing.
3 _____ . Several times.
4 _____ , but I might actually go at the weekend.
5 _____ . I've never really fancied it.
6 _____ . I'd love to, though.
7 _____ . It's great. You should go.
8 _____ . I spent a week there last year.
9 _____ . I'm going this summer, though.
10 _____ . Have you? I've heard it's quite nice.

G For further practice, see Exercise 2 on page 89.

12 Write five questions starting with *Have you (ever) been to …?* Ask about places you know and want to compare experiences of – or places you're thinking of going to and want opinions of.

13 Talk to some other students. Ask your questions and answer other students' questions. Give as many details as you can.

Pompeii

The Tower of London

Hiroshima

Unit 3   Time off   31

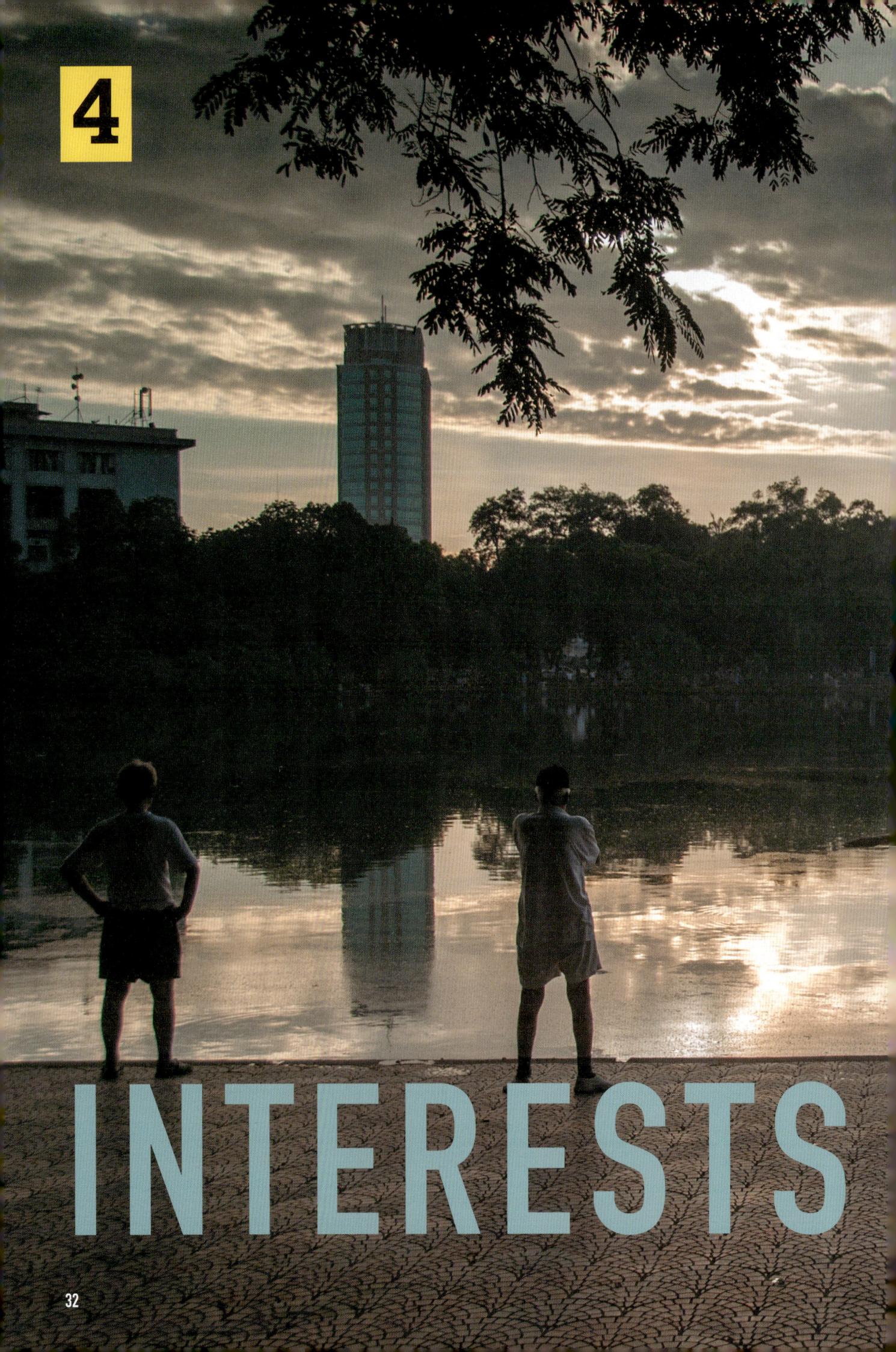

4

INTERESTS

IN THIS UNIT YOU LEARN HOW TO:

- talk about free-time activities
- describe how often you do (or did) things
- explain how good you are at things
- talk about injuries and sports problems
- ask about tastes

SPEAKING

1 **Work in pairs. Discuss the questions.**
   - Where do you think this photo was taken?
   - What time of day do you think it is?
   - Have you ever done anything similar to this? When? Where?
   - Do you do anything to keep fit? What?
   - Are you more of a morning person or a night person?
   - What do you usually do early in the morning and late in the evening?

Unit 4 Interests

MAKING THE MOST OF YOUR TIME

VOCABULARY Free-time activities

1 Match each sentence beginning (1–6) with the two most likely endings (a–l).

1 I went
2 I went to
3 I went for
4 I just stayed in and
5 I had
6 I did

a a run round the block this morning.
b took it easy.
c climbing in the mountains last weekend.
d sailing on a big lake near my house.
e the theatre and saw an amazing play.
f a drive to the beach with my girlfriend on Friday.
g a friend's place for dinner last night.
h a Russian lesson last night.
i some baking for my sister's birthday party.
j played cards with some friends until about two in the morning.
k an early night last night.
l a bit of exercise before breakfast.

2 Work in pairs. Think of one more way to finish each sentence beginning from Exercise 1.

3 Work in groups. Talk about activities in Exercise 1 that you:

1 have done recently.
2 only do occasionally.
3 don't really like doing.
4 have never done.

LISTENING

4 ▶ 18 Listen to three conversations. Answer the questions.

1 Which free-time activities from Exercise 1 do they talk about?
2 How often do Brenda, Domi and Frank do these activities?

5 ▶ 18 Listen again. Are the sentences true (T) or false (F)?

Conversation 1
1 Both speakers have seen the play.
2 One speaker goes to the theatre a lot more often than the other.

Conversation 2
3 The weather wasn't very good at the weekend.
4 Domi went sailing more in the past than now.

Conversation 3
5 Frank had a late night last night.
6 Frank's father doesn't like playing cards.

GRAMMAR

Habit and frequency

To talk about present habits, we use the present simple.

To talk about past habits, we use the past simple or *used to* + infinitive (without *to*).

We use these structures with a range of different frequency phrases.

6 ▶ 19 Work in pairs. Try to remember the missing words from the conversations. Listen and check your ideas.

1 A: So ¹_____ you go to the theatre a ²_____ , then?
   B: Yeah, ³_____ a lot, I guess. Maybe two or three times ⁴_____ month.

2 C: I didn't know you sailed. How ⁵_____ do you do that?
   D: Not as much as I ⁶_____ to, to be honest. When I was living in Brittany, I ⁷_____ all the time, but I ⁸_____ often get the chance now.

3 E: Do you ⁹_____ play poker?
   F: Yeah, quite ¹⁰_____ , actually.

34

7 Underline all the frequency phrases in Exercise 6. Then work in pairs and answer the questions.

1 Which frequency phrase compares now with the past?
2 Which frequency phrases mean the same thing?
3 Do you know any other frequency phrases you could use to answer the questions in Exercise 6?

G Check your ideas on page 89 and do Exercise 1.

8 Complete the frequency phrases with these words.

| all | every | hardly | quite |
| that | used | whenever | would |

1 A: Do you go swimming a lot?
   B: Yeah, **nearly** _____ day, unless I'm really busy.
2 A: Do you eat out a lot?
   B: **Not as much as we** _____ **to**. Before we were married, we went out all the time.
3 A: So do you read much?
   B: Yeah, _____ the time – at least a book a week.
4 A: Do you go to the cinema much?
   B: Yeah, _____ a lot. I probably go once every two weeks.
5 A: How often do you play games on the computer?
   B: **Not** _____ **often, actually**. I don't have time.
6 A: So how often do you go to the gym?
   B: _____ **ever** now, to be honest. Today was the first time in ages. I used to go more often.
7 A: Do you ever try to read in English?
   B: Yeah, _____ **I get the chance**. It's hard to find time, though. Work's so busy.
8 A: Do you ever watch your favourite team play?
   B: Yeah, but **not as much as I** _____ **like to**. I only went four times last season.

PRONUNCIATION

9 ▶20 Listen to the questions in Exercise 8. Practise saying the questions as quickly as you can.

10 Work in groups. Use the questions from Exercise 8 to ask each other about habits. Use frequency phrases to give true answers.

G For further practice, see Exercise 2 on page 90.

DEVELOPING CONVERSATIONS

Are you any good?

We usually use a short phrase to answer the question *Are you any good?* We then explain the phrase in more detail.

A: *I play cards sometimes too. Are you any good?*
B: **Yeah, I'm OK.** *I mean, I'm not a professional or anything, but I enjoy it.*

11 Choose the correct option.

1 a *No, I'm useless. / I'm OK.* I can't even boil an egg.
  b *Yeah, quite good. / No, not really.* I do good soups and I bake quite a lot as well.
2 a *I'm OK. / No, not really.* I used to be OK when I was at school, but I lost interest.
  b *No, I'm useless. / Yeah, quite good.* I usually hit the ball out of the court or into the net.
3 a *Yeah, quite good. / No, not really*. Most people seem to trust me.
  b *I'm OK. / No, I'm useless.* I usually end up telling everybody everything!
4 a *Yeah, quite good. / No, I'm useless.* I mean, I can't even kick a ball in a straight line.
  b *I'm OK. / No, not really.* I didn't enjoy it at school, but now I play tennis quite a lot.

12 Match the questions (a–d) with the four pairs of answers in Exercise 11.

a Are you any good at sport?
b Are you any good at cooking?
c Are you any good at tennis?
d Are you any good at keeping secrets?

13 Write four more *Are you any good at …?* questions. Then work in groups. Ask and answer the questions from Exercise 12 and your own questions.

CONVERSATION PRACTICE

14 Think of a free-time activity that you do quite a lot. Think about how often you do it, where you do it and if you're any good at it. Then have conversations with other students in the class. Use the guide below to help you.

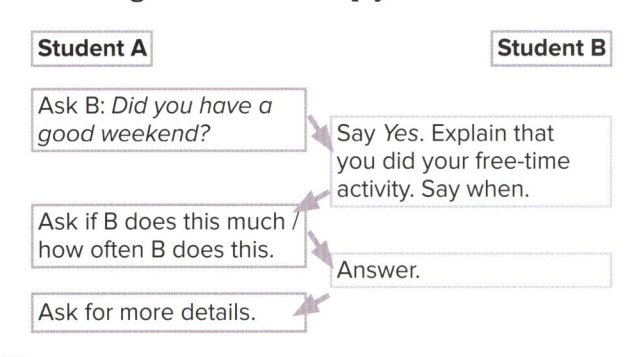

Student A	Student B
Ask B: *Did you have a good weekend?*	
	Say *Yes*. Explain that you did your free-time activity. Say when.
Ask if B does this much / how often B does this.	
	Answer.
Ask for more details.	

6 To watch the video and do the activities, see the DVD ROM.

Unit 4   Interests   35

HIDDEN TALENT

LISTENING

1 Look at the photos of different martial arts on these pages and discuss the questions.
- What do you know about the martial arts in the photos?
- Why do you think people do martial arts?
- What abilities / qualities do you think you need? (e.g. strength, good balance, patience, etc.)
- Do you know anyone who does a martial art? Are they any good?
- What sports did you do at school? Did you like them? Why? / Why not?

2 ▶ 21 Listen to a conversation between Rika and her colleague Ian, who is working in Japan for an international company. Answer the questions.
1 What is the surprising information Ian finds out?
2 Why is he so surprised?
3 Why is Rika annoyed?

3 ▶ 21 Work in pairs. Decide if these sentences about the conversation are true (T) or false (F). Can you remember what Ian and Rika actually said? Listen again and check your ideas.
1 Rika gives someone her autograph.
2 Rika won the judo tournament she entered.
3 You need to be tall to do judo.
4 Rika started doing judo when she was a child.
5 Her teachers at school persuaded her to start doing it.
6 Rika boasts about how good she is.
7 She practises two or three times a week.
8 Rika was once national champion.

4 Work in groups and discuss the questions.
- Do you understand why Rika doesn't talk about her talent at work?
- Do you know anyone who has an unusual hobby or 'hidden' talent? What is it?
- Do you think learning a martial art is the best way to deal with bullying? Why? / Why not? What else could be done?
- Do you know anyone who is very competitive or a bad loser? Give examples.
- Have you ever taken part in a competition? What kind? When? Use some of the phrases below to talk about how well you did.

- I came first / second / 357th / last, etc.
- I lost in the first round / the second round, etc.
- I got to the quarter final / semi-final / final, etc.
- I did it in three hours ten minutes / under an hour, etc.

VOCABULARY Injuries and problems

5 Complete the sentences with these words.

injury	pulled	injured	unfit
confidence	broke	banged	stiff

1 I fell off my bike and _____ my head. Luckily, I was wearing a helmet.
2 I was playing football and _____ my leg. It was in plaster for six weeks.
3 I didn't really warm up before we started playing and so I _____ a muscle in my leg.
4 I'm so _____ ! I went running with a friend, but I had to stop after ten minutes.
5 We did a twenty-mile walk yesterday, so my legs are really _____ this morning.
6 I _____ my back skating. I tried to stand up and I slipped and fell backwards.
7 He beat me 6-0, 6-0. I lost a lot of _____ after that and it took a while to recover.
8 I got a really bad knee _____ a few years ago and it's never really recovered properly.

6 Work in groups. Rank the problems from Exercise 5 from 1 (= most serious) to 8 (= least serious). Explain your decisions.

7 Choose three problems from Exercise 5 that you have experienced. Then work in pairs and tell your partner what happened.

Sanda

Karate

GRAMMAR

Present perfect continuous and past simple for duration

We can use both the present perfect continuous and the past simple to talk about the duration (how long something lasts) of an activity or situation.

8 Look at these extracts from the conversation. Then work in pairs and answer the questions below.

I: *So how long **have** you **been doing** judo, then?* (present perfect continuous)

R: *Ever **since** I was a kid.*

I: *Really? How long **were** you out of action?*

R: *Well, I **didn't do** anything **for** a couple of months.* (past simple)

I: *How long **have** I **known** you now? Six years?* (present perfect simple)

1 Does Rika still do judo?
2 Is Rika still out of action?
3 Does Ian still know Rika?
4 Why don't we say: *How long have I been knowing you now?*
5 What's the difference between *for* and *since*?

G Check your ideas on page 90 and do Exercise 1.

9 ▶22 Respond to these comments by writing a *How long …?* question using the verb in brackets. Then listen and check your answers.

1 It's the first accident he's ever had. He's actually a very good driver. (drive)
2 I can't meet tonight. I have my kickboxing class. (do)
3 I used to be quite good at basketball before I gave up. (play)
4 He only started playing again after the injury two months ago. (be injured)
5 I need to stop. I think I've pulled a muscle. (warm up)
6 My parents are having a party for their wedding anniversary on Saturday. (be married)
7 Her Arabic is pretty good already. (learn)
8 At last! You're here. I was beginning to worry. (wait)

PRONUNCIATION

10 ▶22 Listen again to the questions from Exercise 9. Notice the contractions and weak forms of *have, has, been, did, you,* etc. when we speak fast. Practise saying the questions as quickly as you can.

11 Work in pairs. Have eight conversations starting with the comments and questions from Exercise 9. Continue each conversation for as long as you can.

A: *It's the first accident he's ever had. He's actually a very good driver.*
B: *I'm sure. How long has he been driving?*
A: *About five or six years.*
B: *Right. So how did the accident happen?*
A: *This car didn't stop at the lights and crashed into him.*
B: *Oh dear.*

G For further practice, see Exercise 2 on page 91.

SPEAKING

12 Work in groups. Find the answers to the questions below for your group. Find out two more details, such as *how long, when, where, how often, why* or *how*.

1 Who is the fittest person?
2 Who has run the longest distance?
3 Who has given up a hobby or sport?
4 Who plays a musical instrument well?
5 Who has got to this level of English the quickest?
6 Who has done the last homework the teacher gave you?
7 Who has been on the longest journey?
8 Who has experienced the longest wait for a plane or train?
9 Who has lived in their house for the shortest time?
10 Who has seen the longest film?
11 Who had the shortest journey to get here?

Judo

Kalaripayattu

Unit 4   Interests   37

THE SOUNDTRACK OF OUR LIVES

VOCABULARY Describing music

1 Check you understand the adjectives in bold in the sentences below. Think of songs or genres of music you could describe using these adjectives.

1 If a song is **catchy**, you quickly want to sing it and can't stop.
2 If music is **repetitive**, it has the same boom boom beat all the way through.
3 If a song is **heavy**, it's very loud and has a strong beat.
4 If a song is **soft**, it's quiet and relaxing to listen to.
5 If we say the music or lyrics (the words to the song) are **sentimental**, they are romantic or sad in a bad way.
6 If we say a song is very **commercial**, it is a negative way of saying it is written to sell a lot.
7 If music or songs are **moving**, they make you cry.
8 If music is **bland**, it's boring.
9 If music is **uplifting**, it makes you happy or hopeful.
10 If music is **depressing**, it makes you sad.

2 Work in pairs and compare your ideas. Say whether or not you like the songs / genres you thought of and explain why.

DEVELOPING CONVERSATIONS

Talking about tastes
We often move from asking about general tastes to more specific tastes. There are common questions we ask when talking about music, films and books.

3 Put the conversation into the correct order. The first one is done for you.

a Erm, I don't know ... Girls Rock, Soul Train, **stuff like that**.
b **All sorts really, but mainly** pop music and R&B.
c Oh right. **Anyone in particular?**
d Yeah, all the time.
e So **have you** heard **anything good recently?**
f **What kind of** music **are you into?**
g **Do you** listen to music **much?**   1
h Well, I downloaded this great song by K Boy. It's fantastic.

4 ▶ 23 Listen and check your answers.

5 Talk to other students and have similar conversations about music, films and books. Try to use some of the expressions in bold from Exercise 3.

READING

6 Work in pairs. Look at the song titles and artists below. Do you know any of them? Do you like them?

- *Hey Jude* (The Beatles)
- *Stuck Me* (The Gimmies)
- *Starships* (Nicki Minaj)
- *The Four Seasons* (Vivaldi)
- *Limón Y Sal* (Julieta Venegas)
- *I Wanna Be Like You* (from *The Jungle Book*)
- *Take My Hand* (Ivan & The Parazol)
- *My Heart Will Go On* (Céline Dion)
- *Gangnam Style* (Psy)

7 Read the article and find out if the readers like the songs in Exercise 6 or not – and why.

8 Read the article again. Which person / people in the article:

1 likes different kinds of music to their father?
2 finds some songs drive them mad?
3 has good memories of time spent abroad?
4 went to a concert by one of their favourite bands?
5 predicts that one band will become famous?
6 mention special ceremonies?

9 Correct the words in italics with words from the article. Then work in pairs. Discuss if any of the sentences are true for you.

1 There's a song I dance to whenever it *puts* on in a club.
2 If I'm sad, I like to play something sad to *same* my mood.
3 I love singing *together* to songs. I like karaoke.
4 I've seen lots of bands *lively*.
5 I don't like *sensitive* songs about love and romance.
6 There's a song which really *remembers* me of my father.
7 I sometimes *make* stupid dances to some songs.
8 I like to study with music on in the *behind*.
9 Classical music doesn't *feel* anything for me. It's bland.

10 With your partner, discuss which person in the article you are most / least similar to – and why.

SPEAKING

11 Choose two playlist titles from below and make a list of three songs you want to include.

- My current favourites
- That reminds me of ...
- Party music
- Music I can't stand
- Music to fall asleep to
- Music for a romantic evening
- I can't get it out of my head

12 Work in groups and compare your lists. Say as much as you can about the songs you have chosen. Ask extra questions to continue each conversation.

38

THE PLAYLIST OF YOUR LIFE

For generations, music lovers have made collections of songs to soundtrack their lives. Nowadays, technology makes it easier than ever to create, find and share playlists to suit every mood and occasion. We set our readers 'a playlist challenge'. Here is their response.

THAT WAS A GREAT YEAR PLAYLIST

Starships by Nicki Minaj reminds me of 2012, which I spent studying in Amsterdam. There were loads of other foreigners studying there and we became very close. We all worked hard, but we partied hard as well. Whenever this song came on at a party or club, we all jumped up and danced – it didn't matter how tired we were. There's a great video that goes with it too. I sometimes watch it online. *[Corina, Germany]*

Good Feeling	FLO RIDA
Levels	AVICII
Bom Bom	SAM & THE WOMP
Don't You Worry Child	SWEDISH HOUSE MAFIA
NOW PLAYING Starships	NICKI MINAJ

MUSIC WHEN I'M DOWN PLAYLIST

I've put Vivaldi's *The Four Seasons*, but I actually only play two seasons! The winter section is sad and moving and that sometimes matches my mood, but then I play the spring section because it's so uplifting. I'd actually like it played at my funeral! There was life before me, there will be life after me, like spring that comes again after winter.
Julieta Venegas' *Limón Y Sal* also cheers me up. My husband bought it for me. The lyrics basically say 'I love you however you are; you don't have to change anything.' *[Kari, Chile]*

The Four Seasons	VIVALDI
NOW PLAYING Limón Y Sal	JULIETA VENEGAS
Bridge Over Troubled Water	SIMON & GARFUNKEL
Happy	THE ROLLING STONES
Someone Special	POETS OF THE FALL

ALL-TIME CLASSICS PLAYLIST

The top of any all-time classic list has to be *Hey Jude* by the Beatles. It's a song you immediately want to sing along to. The Beatles are the reason why I learnt English. *Stuck Me* is by The Gimmies, a Japanese band. I've seen them live and they were loud and energetic – incredible. *[Toshi, Japan]*

Hey Jude	THE BEATLES
Stuck Me	THE GIMMIES
NOW PLAYING Communication Breakdown	LED ZEPPELIN
I Feel Good	THEEE BAT
Shake Some Action	THE FLAMIN' GROOVIES

MUSIC FOR MY WORST ENEMY PLAYLIST

This was difficult to choose. I hate that Céline Dion song that was used in the film *Titanic – My Heart Will Go On*. I can't stand commercial pop music – it's so sentimental. However, the worst is *Gangnam Style* by Psy. It reminds me of family weddings and people doing the stupid dance. The problem is it's so catchy! The other day I heard it as the ringtone on a mobile phone and I couldn't get it out of my head all morning! It was really annoying. *[Kevin, Scotland]*

My Heart Will Go On	CÉLINE DION
Gangnam Style	PSY
The Hamster Dance	HAMPTON THE HAMSTER
The Final Countdown	EUROPE
Superstar	TOY BOX

MY FAMILY PLAYLIST

My dad's a big jazz fan and always has music on in the background. Personally, jazz doesn't do anything for me. I just find it strange. However, he used to play one song for me – *I Wanna Be Like You* from the film *The Jungle Book*. Now we play it to my younger brother and it always makes him laugh.
Take my Hand is for my sister. We both love indie music and it's by a relatively new Hungarian band called Ivan & The Parazol that we've been listening to a lot recently. They're going to be big. *[Natalia, Hungary]*

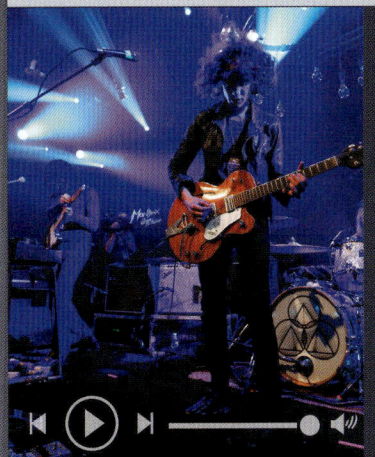

I Wanna Be Like You	LOUIS PRIMA
Take My Hand	IVAN & THE PARAZOL
A Love Supreme	JOHN COLTRANE
NOW PLAYING Move With The Season	TEMPLES
Not Quite Right	WOHLLEBE

Unit 4   Interests   39

VIDEO 2

WORLD HERITAGE QUIZ

2 Read this short article and find the answers to the questions in Exercise 1.

> The idea of creating a list of World Heritage Sites began in the 1950s when the ancient ruins of Abu Simbel in Egypt were in danger from a plan to build a dam and create a huge lake. The lake was going to flood the Abu Simbel Temple and destroy it. However, several countries worked together to save the temples by cutting them up and moving them to higher ground. The work involved archaeologists, engineers and financial support from a number of governments internationally. After this, an agreement was signed by many countries to protect places which are very important culturally or environmentally. Since the 1970s, almost 1,000 places have been listed. These include islands, lakes, mountains and rivers, and everything from cave paintings to Roman ruins, medieval towns to churches and mosques, and even early industrial buildings. The list is managed by the United Nations organisation UNESCO.

3 ▶ 7 You are going to do a quiz. Work in teams. Watch the video and make notes to answer the twelve questions you hear.

4 ▶ 8 Watch the video to find the answers. Write one new piece of information you hear for each. The winner is the team with the most points, but if it's a draw, the team with the most extra information wins.

5 Work in groups. Discuss the questions.
- Which three places would you most like to visit? Why?
- Are there any you wouldn't want to visit? Why?
- Do you know any other World Heritage Sites? Why are they World Heritage Sites? Have you been to them?
- What would you recommend as a new World Heritage Site? Why?

1 Work in pairs. Look at the photos and discuss the questions.
- Do you know where it is?
- What do you think happened here? Why?
- Do you know what World Heritage Sites are and who manages the list?
- What kinds of places are included on the list?

REVIEW 2

GRAMMAR

1 Complete the text with one word in each space.

In March, I'm ¹_____ to Taghazout in Morocco for a holiday. I'm really ²_____ surfing, and it's supposed ³_____ be one of the best places for surfing in the world. I've been surfing ⁴_____ about five years now, but nowhere that has big waves like they do in Taghazout, so I'm looking forward to testing myself. A friend of mine is thinking ⁵_____ coming with me, but he still hasn't ⁶_____ . We've known each other ⁷_____ we were kids, but he only started surfing a few months ⁸_____ , so he feels he's not quite ready. I've told him he could go sightseeing instead as there are lots of interesting places all ⁹_____ the area. It's warm and sunny ¹⁰_____ every day at that time of year, so he could just lie on the beach and get a suntan.

2 Complete the second sentence so that it has a similar meaning to the first sentence using the word given. Do not change the word given. You must use between four and five words, including the word given.

1. Before I started work, I read a lot more.
   I don't read as _____ . **USED**
2. I go to the gym as much as I can.
   I go to the gym _____ . **CHANCE**
3. I joined the club ten years ago now.
   I _____ of the club for ten years now. **MEMBER**
4. We might go to see a show while we're there.
   We _____ to see a show while we're there. **ARE**
5. I've never been there, but I've heard it's great.
   I haven't been there, but it _____ great. **BE**
6. When did you start working here?
   How _____ here now? **WORKING**

3 Choose the correct option.

1. A: Have you ever been to Europe?
   B: Yeah, I *spent / have spent* some time in Spain a few years ago.
2. A: What's the forecast for tomorrow?
   B: They said it's *going to rain / raining* most of the day.
3. A: *Do you have / Are you having* any plans for the weekend?
   B: Yeah. *We're going to / We will* visit some friends who live in Milan.
4. A: *Do you go / Are you going* to the cinema much?
   B: Hardly *never / ever*. I usually just watch them on my computer.
5. A: I *played / was playing* basketball a lot but I gave up after I injured my knee.
   B: How long *have you played? / did you play for?*
6. A: *Do you ever eat out? / Have you ever eaten out?*
   B: Quite often – maybe once *a / every* couple of months.

4 ▶24 Listen and write the six sentences you hear.

5 Write a sentence before and after the sentences from Exercise 4 to create short dialogues.

VOCABULARY

6 Match the verbs (1–8) with the collocates (a–h).

1. go   a. Roman ruins / a royal palace
2. go for   b. sailing / climbing
3. pour   c. by fire / in a storm
4. hire   d. my head / my leg
5. restore   e. with rain / down
6. match   f. my mood / the description
7. bang   g. a bike / a boat
8. be destroyed h. a meal / a run

7 Decide if these words and phrases are connected to places of interest, weather or sport.

blow away	injure	gallery	stiff
lively	miserable	humid	freezing
unfit	medieval	warm up	stalls

8 Complete the sentences. Use the word in brackets to form a word that fits in the space.

1. It was absolutely _____ last month so I'm glad it's cooling down now. (boil)
2. It's going to be nice and sunny, so we could go _____ , if you like. (fish)
3. My first _____ when I heard it was to start dancing. (react)
4. It was a bit embarrassing because I'm _____ at dancing. (use)
5. I can't get that song out of my head, it's so _____ . (catch)
6. I don't listen to much pop music. I find it too _____ . (repeat)
7. She thought the film was really _____ , but I thought it was too _____ . (move, sentiment)
8. Since I had my _____ I've lost quite a lot of _____ . (injure, confident)

9 Complete the text with one word in each space. The first letters are given.

I went to Istanbul on holiday last year. We were a bit stupid, because we didn't check the weather ¹fo_____ before we went – we just assumed it was going to be ²bo_____ hot. When we arrived though, it was quite ³gr_____ and cloudy and at night it turned out to be quite ⁴ch_____ . We ended up going to a street market to buy some extra clothes! The city itself was fantastic. We stayed in the old ⁵di_____ where you have the Topkapi ⁶Pa_____ where the Sultan lived and we went to see and pray in the famous Blue ⁷Mo_____ . We also went up the Galata ⁸To_____ which had fantastic views over the city. And also to Taksim Square, where there is a monument that ⁹co_____ the foundation of the Turkish Republic. There was also great ¹⁰ni_____ in and around Taksim. We stayed out till five in the morning one night. And I loved that mixture of old and new. We went to a quite trendy restaurant which had a glass floor over some ruins from the fifth ¹¹ce_____ . I'll definitely go there again. Even the weather ¹²cl_____ u_____ by the end of our week and it was lovely and sunny.

Review 2   41

5

IN THIS UNIT YOU LEARN HOW TO:

- talk about jobs and what they involve
- comment on people's experiences
- discuss rules and freedoms at work
- talk about getting used to changes
- say longer chunks better

SPEAKING

1 Work in pairs. Look at the photo and discuss the questions.

- What do you think the people are doing?
- Where do you think it is? Why?
- What might be good or bad about this job?

2 Work in groups. Which of these jobs are needed to get the tea leaves in the photo to a person drinking the same tea in another country? Explain why each job is needed.

labourer	graphic designer	trader
engineer	programmer	surgeon
truck driver	electrician	sales rep
civil servant	lawyer	security guard
plumber	accountant	estate agent

WORKING LIFE

Unit 5 Working life

THAT MUST BE STRESSFUL

VOCABULARY Describing jobs

1 Work in pairs. Check you understand the words and phrases in bold in the sentences below. Then think of one job that each sentence could describe.

1 It's very **competitive**. Lots of people want to get into that **field** and hundreds of people **apply for** each job.
2 It's very **well-paid**. He gets £60,000 a year as well as a **bonus** at the end of the year.
3 It's quite **rewarding**. You really help people and that makes you feel good.
4 It's quite **insecure**. You're either **self-employed** or have a **temporary contract** and it's quite badly paid.
5 It's **easy**. You don't have any real **responsibility** like managing anyone. You do the job, go home and forget about it.
6 You need to be quite **creative**. You have to think of a lot of new ideas and new ways of doing things.
7 It's very **stressful**. You're **under a lot of time pressure**.
8 Physically, it's very **demanding**. You have to be strong and fit.
9 It's very **varied**. You get to do lots of different things.
10 It's a bit **dull**. It mainly involves **admin** and **paperwork**. I basically sit at a desk all day.

2 Work in pairs. Answer the questions.

1 What's involved in applying for a job?
2 What's the opposite of well-paid?
3 Why might someone get a bonus?
4 What other important responsibilities might a job have?
5 What's the opposite of a temporary contract?
6 What kinds of things might admin involve?

3 Work in groups. Look at the jobs on page 43 and discuss these questions.

- Are the jobs good or bad jobs to have in your country at the moment? Why?
- Do any of your friends or family do any of these jobs?
- Who do they work for? Do they enjoy it?

LISTENING

4 ▶ 25 Listen to two people – Amanda and Ivan – who have recently met. Answer the questions.

1 What do they do now?
2 What jobs have they done in the past?
3 What are Ivan's plans for the future? Why?
4 How old are they both now?

5 ▶ 25 Choose the correct option. Then listen again and check your answers.

1 I'm involved *in / on* designing what you see on the screen.
2 How did you *getting / get* into that?
3 Vodafone were recruiting people so I *applied / replied* and I got a job.
4 It's like any job. It has its boring *moments / minutes*.
5 It depends if we have a deadline to *complete / meet*.
6 That *can't / can* be easy.
7 I sometimes work better *under / in* pressure.

6 Work in pairs. Discuss the questions.

- What do you think of Amanda's job? Would you be any good at it? Why? / Why not?
- Would you ever work for little or no money like Ivan?
- Are there any jobs for life in your country? Do you think having a job for life is good?

DEVELOPING CONVERSATIONS

Doing what?

When people reply to the question *What do you do?* by talking about their company, place of employment or department, we often try to find out exactly what work they do by asking *Doing what?* Notice the other useful phrases in bold in the extract below:

I: *So what do you do, Amanda?*
A: **I work for** *a mobile phone company.*
I: *Oh yeah.* **Doing what?**
A: **I work in** *the design* **department**. **I'm involved in** *designing what you see on the screen.*

7 Match the jobs (1–5) with the specific job descriptions (a–e).

1 I work in the warehouse.
2 I'm in the accounts department.
3 I work in human resources.
4 I'm in sales.
5 I work in the marketing department.

a **I mainly do** admin, but sometimes **I'm involved in** planning the campaigns.
b **I'm the rep for** the whole of the south of Italy.
c **I do** all the orders and get them ready for the delivery.
d **I'm responsible for** recruitment contracts and working conditions.
e **I deal with** all the pay and finances.

8 Use the language from the box above and Exercise 7 to have five conversations starting with *What do you do?*

GRAMMAR
Must and *can't* for commenting

9 Look at these extracts from the conversation. Then choose the correct option to complete the rules in the Grammar box.

A: *I was 25 when I joined, so eight years. Time goes so fast!*
I: *You* **must enjoy** *it.*
A: *Yeah, I* **do** *generally. It* **'s** *quite varied.*

A: *Sometimes I do something like fifty or sixty hours a week.*
I: *Really? That* **can't be** *easy.*
A: *It* **'s** *actually fine. I mean, it* **is** *a bit stressful sometimes, but you* **get** *used to it.*

I: *It's almost a job for life.*
A: *Really? That* **must be** *very competitive.*
I: *Yeah, it* **is**.

We often use *must* and *can't* + infinitive (without *to*) to comment on other people's experiences and feelings. *Must* and *can't* show that we think our comments are [1] *definitely true / probably true*, but we're not 100% sure.

In sentences with a positive meaning, we use [2] *must / can't*.
In sentences with a negative meaning, we use [3] *must / can't*.

When we respond to comments using *must* or *can't*, we [4] *often use / don't often use* the present simple. This shows we [5] *know / believe* but aren't sure these things are true.

When responding, we [6] *usually / don't often* repeat the verbs and adjectives used in the comments.

G Check your ideas on page 91 and do Exercise 1.

10 Write comments on these sentences using *must* and *can't*.

1 I'm the sales manager for Europe. I'm in charge of thirty reps.
2 I travel a lot round Europe and the Middle East.
3 I care for people who are dying.
4 His wife's a tax lawyer for a top accountancy company.
5 I really see my students develop and improve.
6 Basically, I just sit in front of a screen all day.
7 I don't have any work after this contract comes to an end next month.
8 They said they're going to give us all a bonus.

PRONUNCIATION

11 ▶ 26 Listen to some possible comments on the sentences in Exercise 10. Notice how we often don't pronounce the '*t*' in *must* or *can't*.

12 ▶ 26 Listen to the comments again and repeat.

13 Work in pairs. Practise having three-part conversations starting with the sentences from Exercise 10.

A: *I'm the sales manager for Europe. I'm in charge of thirty reps.*
B: *That must be interesting.*
A: *It is. I really love it.*

G For further practice, see Exercise 2 on page 92.

CONVERSATION PRACTICE

14 Choose one of these tasks.

a Work in pairs. Think of two jobs each. Take turns to use language from this lesson to describe the job without saying what it is. Your partner should guess the job.

b Have conversations with other students and find out about their jobs. Use language from this lesson. Comment on what others say using *must* or *can't* at least once.

9 To watch the video and do the activities, see the DVD ROM.

Unit 5 Working life 45

IT'S AGAINST THE RULES

LISTENING

1 Look at the sentences below about rules at work. Then work in groups and discuss these questions.

- Why do you think companies have these rules?
- Do you think they are sensible and fair?

1 Women have to wear skirts or dresses at work.
2 We have to agree holidays with our boss. We can't just take time off when we want.
3 We have to ask the admin assistant to make photocopies for us. We can't just do them ourselves.
4 We have to take our breaks at set times.
5 We have to wear a hard hat at all times.
6 We can't surf the web on company computers.
7 We can't install any software on the company's computers.
8 We can't talk to each other while we're working.
9 We can't wear watches in the warehouse.
10 We can work from home one day a week.

2 ▶27 Listen to three conversations about rules at work. Match each conversation (A–C) to one of the rules in Exercise 1.

3 ▶27 Choose the correct option. Then listen again and check your answers.

1 Apparently, he's been given a *writing / written* warning.
2 He was always sending *person / personal* emails.
3 He somehow got a computer virus and then it infected the *whole / all* system.
4 I've got this new job working in a *law / lawyer* firm.
5 What if you can't wear something for *religion / religious* or health reasons?
6 I don't know. I guess they *make / give* an exception.
7 Can I have a *quick / fast* word?
8 Listen, I'd like to take the day *out / off* on Friday.
9 I've asked you at *short / recent* notice before and it hasn't been a problem.

4 Work in pairs. Who do you have more sympathy with in each conversation – the company or the workers? Why?

GRAMMAR

Talking about rules

When we talk about rules we generally use *have to, can / can't, be (not) allowed to, be (not) supposed to*. We prefer to use these forms instead of *must / mustn't* because *must / mustn't* can sound too direct and rude.

5 Look at these sentences from the conversations. Complete the statements below with the structures in bold.

a We're certainly **allowed to** do it in our breaks.
b Apparently, you're **not allowed to** use the company computers like that.
c You **can't** even wear smart trousers.
d You **have to** wear skirts!
e You're **supposed to** arrange time off with me a month in advance.

1 We often use _____ or _____ instead of *must*.
2 We often use _____ or _____ instead of *mustn't*.
3 We often use _____ instead of *can*.
4 We often use _____ when the rule has just been broken or is often not followed.

G Check your ideas on page 92 and do Exercise 1.

6 Replace the words in italics with the correct form of *be allowed to, be supposed to* or *have to*.

1 One other rule we have is that you *mustn't smoke* on any part of the company property – inside or outside.
2 Is there a dress code? *Can I wear* make-up or jewellery?
3 I *mustn't help* you. It's against the rules, but for you, I'll make an exception.
4 Our contract says we *must be* in the office a minimum of 35 hours a week. They're very strict about it.
5 *Must you work* at weekends, if the company asks you to?
6 Other people *can't work* from home, but they made an exception in my case because of my heart problem.
7 We sometimes *must work* late or at the weekend, but we *can take* time off the following week if we do.
8 I'm sorry, but only senior staff *can use* these toilets. You *must go* to the ones downstairs.

7 Work in pairs. Decide if you are going to talk about rules where you work, where you study or at home. First, work on your own and think of the following:
- two rules you like / don't like – and why
- two rules which are often broken
- two questions for your partner about rules where they work / study

Now work with your partner, compare your ideas and ask each other questions.

G For further practice, see Exercise 2 on page 92.

VOCABULARY Work rules and laws

8 Complete the sentences below with these pairs of words. Underline the other words that go with each word. The first one is done for you.

against + discrimination	fined + ignored
banned + unpopular	changed + fire
breaking + fine	~~requirement + enforce~~
court + won	introduced + reduce

1 It is actually <u>a legal</u> *requirement* to pay the minimum wage, but the government <u>doesn't do enough to</u> *enforce* <u>the law</u>.
2 The company was found guilty of _____ environmental laws so they had to pay a huge _____ .
3 The company _____ the use of social media during work hours, which was quite an _____ decision.
4 The government has _____ employment laws, so it is easier for companies to hire and _____ people.
5 The company was _____ because it had _____ health and safety rules and had put its workers at risk.
6 The workers took the company to _____ because they had been exposed to dangerous chemicals and they _____ their case.
7 They recently _____ new rules about accepting gifts because they're trying to _____ corruption.
8 It's _____ the law to discriminate against women, but it doesn't mean that _____ doesn't still happen at work.

9 Work in pairs. Discuss the questions.
- Have you heard of any companies being taken to court? Who by? Why? Who won the case?
- What employment laws do you know? Do you think they are good? Why? / Why not?
- How strict are health and safety rules in your country? Is that good or bad? Why?
- Would you like to see any rules / laws introduced or relaxed? Which ones? Why?
- Is there much discrimination in your country? Against who?

'No, I did not have a good day at the office, you know that's against the rules.'

Unit 5 Working life **47**

SOMEONE HAS TO DO IT

READING

1 Work in groups. Read the introduction of the magazine article below and discuss the questions.
- How much free time do you have? Is it more or less than in the past? Why?
- Give an example of one terrible job from the past that has disappeared. Why do you think it disappeared?
- Think of one job where you:
  - risk injury.
  - are exposed to chemicals or dirt.
  - might die of boredom.

2 Read the rest of the article about four terrible modern jobs. Match the sentences below to the jobs. Sometimes there is more than one possible answer. Underline the parts of the article that help you decide. Then work in pairs and compare your ideas.
a The hours are very long.
b Someone had a good relationship with their co-workers.
c People shout at and insult the workers.
d The workers risk catching a disease.
e Someone has an injury as the result of work.
f Someone feels stuck in their job.
g Someone finds the work rewarding.
h People are paid quite well for the hours they do.

3 Rank the jobs in the article from 1 (= best) to 4 (= worst). Then work in groups. Compare your lists and explain your decisions.

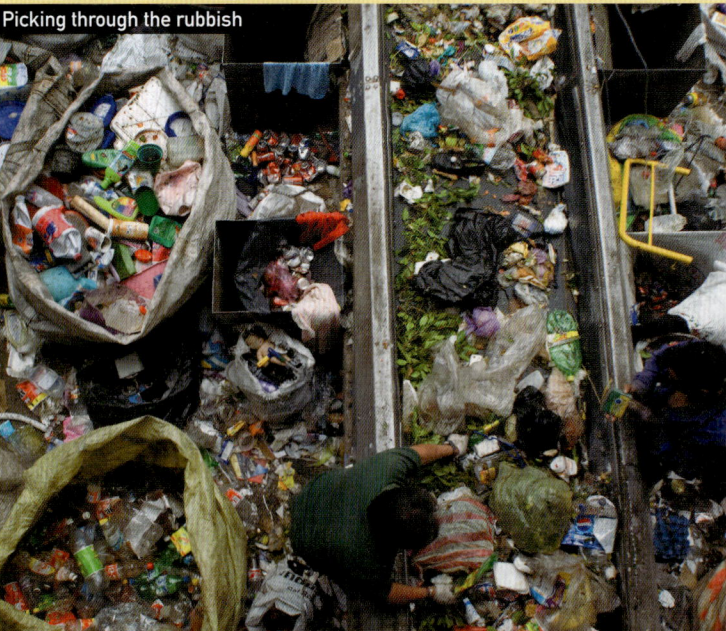

TERRIBLE JOBS
NOT A THING OF THE PAST

For over a century, people have been predicting that technology would give us more free time: we could eat pills instead of cooking, robots would clean our houses, the Internet would mean none of us would have to waste time travelling to work. Technology would also solve other nasty problems, so no-one would have to do dangerous, dirty or dull work to earn money. That was the prediction! Sadly, it's not quite worked out that way. In many countries, people are working more hours than fifty years ago. Some terrible jobs may have disappeared: for example, we don't make the colour purple with rotting seafood anymore! However, there are still plenty of bad jobs left – jobs in which you may risk injury, be exposed to chemicals and dirt or maybe just die of boredom!

1 HUMAN GUINEA PIG

Hundreds of people take part in drug trials every year. For between €45 and €4,500, they take a new drug to test for any side effects, such as vomiting or headaches. Some students join these drug trials as a relatively quick and easy way of earning money. John Spiral, a history student from Dublin, regularly does them. 'You might go to the hospital three or four times, maybe eight hours 'work'. I had a really upset stomach once, and another time I got strange red marks on my skin, but that's all. Usually it's fine, and you're helping science, which benefits everyone!'

2 EMBALMER

Embalmers preserve dead bodies in preparation for funerals. They work anything up to 50 hours a week for a salary of around £15,000 a year, far less than the national average. They spend most of the day on their feet and generally work bent over a table. They also have to work with very strong-smelling chemicals. 'I suffer from backache, but the job's not as bad as you might think,' says Frank McCreary. 'I'm even used to the smell now – I don't even notice it. And of course the families of the dead are usually very grateful for the job I've done, which is obviously a big motivation for me.'

Stress-reducing plants in a Chinese call centre

Picking through the rubbish

4 The chunks in bold below are all used in the article. Find the missing words to complete them.

1. The company has developed **a relatively _____ and _____ way of** treating the disease.
2. I'm taking a course _____ **preparation** _____ the civil service exams.
3. Working in the warehouse **is not as bad as you** _____ _____ . We have some fun.
4. Apparently, even low _____ _____ **stress** can increase the risk of heart attacks.
5. I've been rushing around so much, I've **had** _____ _____ **to think** about this meeting.
6. I'm working in a factory **for** _____ **minimum** _____ , so I can't afford to rent a flat on my own.
7. I'm surprised she's decided to accept a job there. She **could** _____ **better** _____ **herself**!

5 Work in pairs. Discuss the questions.

- What quick and easy ways of making money do you think there are?
- What are the three most important things you should learn in preparation for adult life?
- Do you know what the minimum wage is in your country? What do you think of it?
- Do you know anyone who could do better for themselves? In what way?

3 CALL CENTRE WORKER

Many banks and other companies have call centres abroad where customers can ring for information or to complain. Levels of stress among workers are very high. They often work in cramped conditions, have to stare at a computer all day, and have little opportunity to laugh or joke with their co-workers.

One worker, from an Indian call centre, said, 'We get quite a lot of abuse. I can't repeat what some people scream at us. Often there is nothing you can do about their complaint, so they slam down the phone, but then you have no time to think before another person calls you straightaway. I don't think I'll ever get used to it. I'd like to leave, but the money's quite good and there's a lot of competition for jobs here in Mumbai.'

4 RECYCLING PLANT WORKER

You're supposed to sort your own rubbish and put glass in one bag, paper in another, but unfortunately many people still don't do this. So workers in a recycling plant have to find the recyclable items from a big pile of rubbish, and all for the minimum wage. 'You're just dirty all the time and you go home smelling,' says Solomon Iwenofu, an ex-plant worker. 'I got used to it after a while, but my wife never did!' Apart from the smell, there are dangers in handling everything from dirty nappies to rotting meat and used syringes. 'I got on really well with my co-workers and we often joked about things we found, but we also knew you can get hepatitis or other serious illnesses if you're not careful.' Luckily for Solomon, it was only a temporary job. 'It helped me when I first came to America, but I always knew I could do better for myself and my family.'

UNDERSTANDING VOCABULARY

Be used to and get used to

Be used to shows a habit or situation is normal for us because of our experience, but others might think of it as difficult. *Be used to* can be followed by a noun or an *-ing* form.

I'm even *used to the smell* now – I don't even notice it.

Get used to shows a change from being difficult to becoming normal or easy.

I **got used to it** after a while, but my wife never did!

6 Complete the exchanges by putting the words in brackets into the correct order.

1. A: It must be difficult getting up so early.
   B: Oh, _____ (to / I'm / it / used). I had to get up at five in my last job.
2. A: How are you finding the new job?
   B: It is difficult, but _____ (getting / slowly / to / it / I'm / used). The people I work with are being very supportive.
3. A: How are you finding your new job?
   B: Not that good, to be honest. I hate sitting at a desk all day, but I need the money, so I guess _____ (to / I'll / get / used / to / just / have / it).
4. A: How do you find working shifts?
   B: OK, although it _____ (get / to / me / a / while / used / took / to) working nights. I couldn't sleep during the day to begin with, but it's fine now.
5. A: How do you find working nights? It must be quite difficult.
   B: It was to begin with, yeah, but _____ (it / totally / now / I'm / to / used).
6. A: How are you finding your new job?
   B: The job's OK, but I hate the journey to work. _____ (I'll / think / don't / ever / I / used / to / get) the crowded trains!

PRONUNCIATION

7 ▶ 28 When learning to say longer chunks, it helps to say them a bit at a time, starting from the end. Listen to and then repeat *I guess I'll have to get used to it* divided into bits.

8 Practise saying the other *be used to* and *get used to* phrases in Exercise 6. Then work in pairs and practise reading out the exchanges.

SPEAKING

9 Think about the biggest change you have had in your life. Make notes about the following. Then work in groups and tell your stories.

- when and why it happened
- how you felt about the change
- what was good about the change
- what was difficult and how you got used to it
- how you feel about that change now

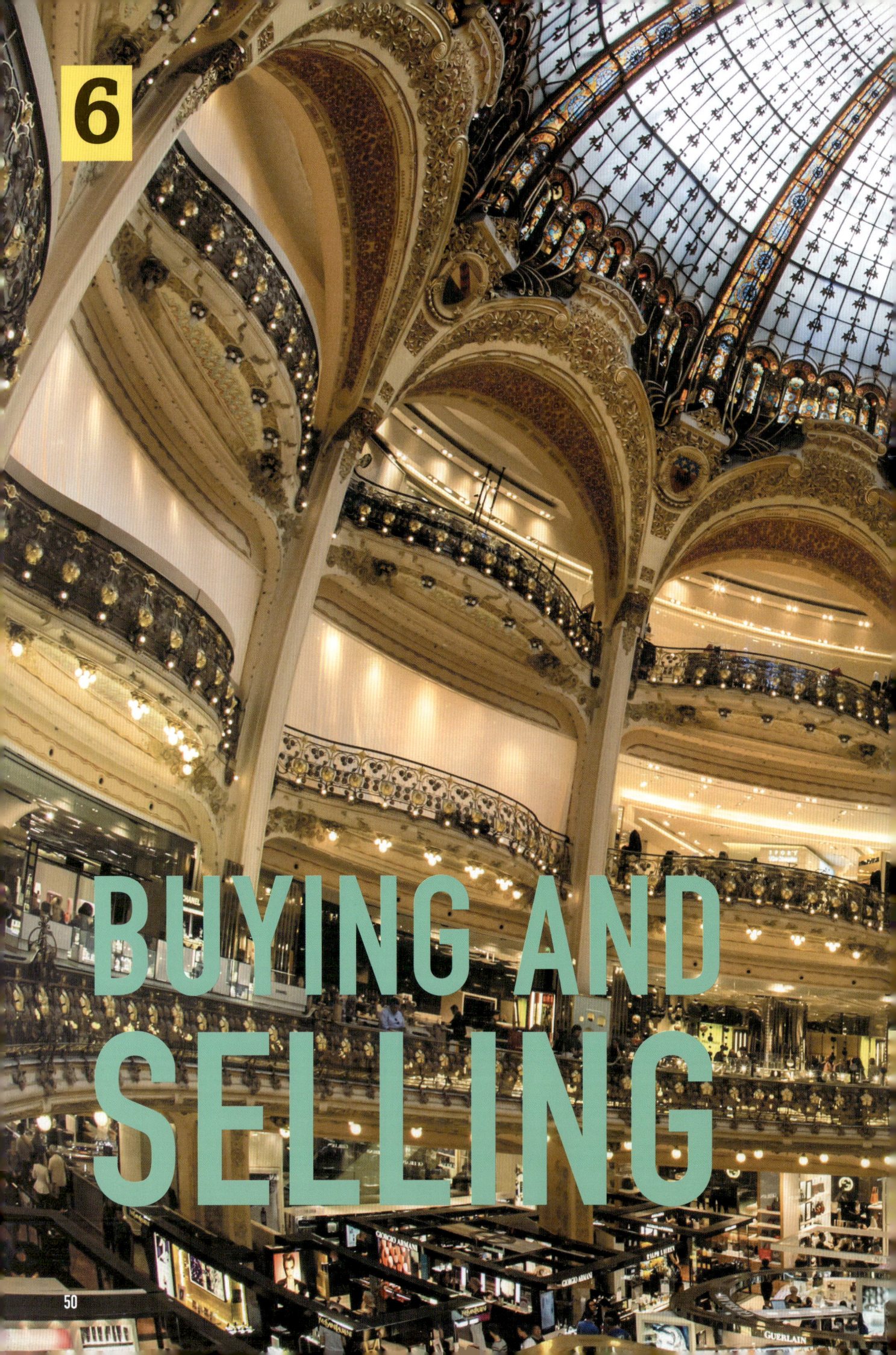

6

BUYING AND SELLING

IN THIS UNIT YOU LEARN HOW TO:

- talk about phones and phone companies
- compare products
- describe what people are wearing
- discuss shopping habits
- describe souvenirs and presents
- negotiate a good price

SPEAKING

1 Work in pairs. Look at the photo and discuss the questions.
- Where do you think this photo was taken?
- Do you have any places like this where you live? Do you ever go there?
- What do you think is good / bad about shopping in a place like this?
- What kinds of things do you most / least like shopping for?
- What was the last thing you bought?

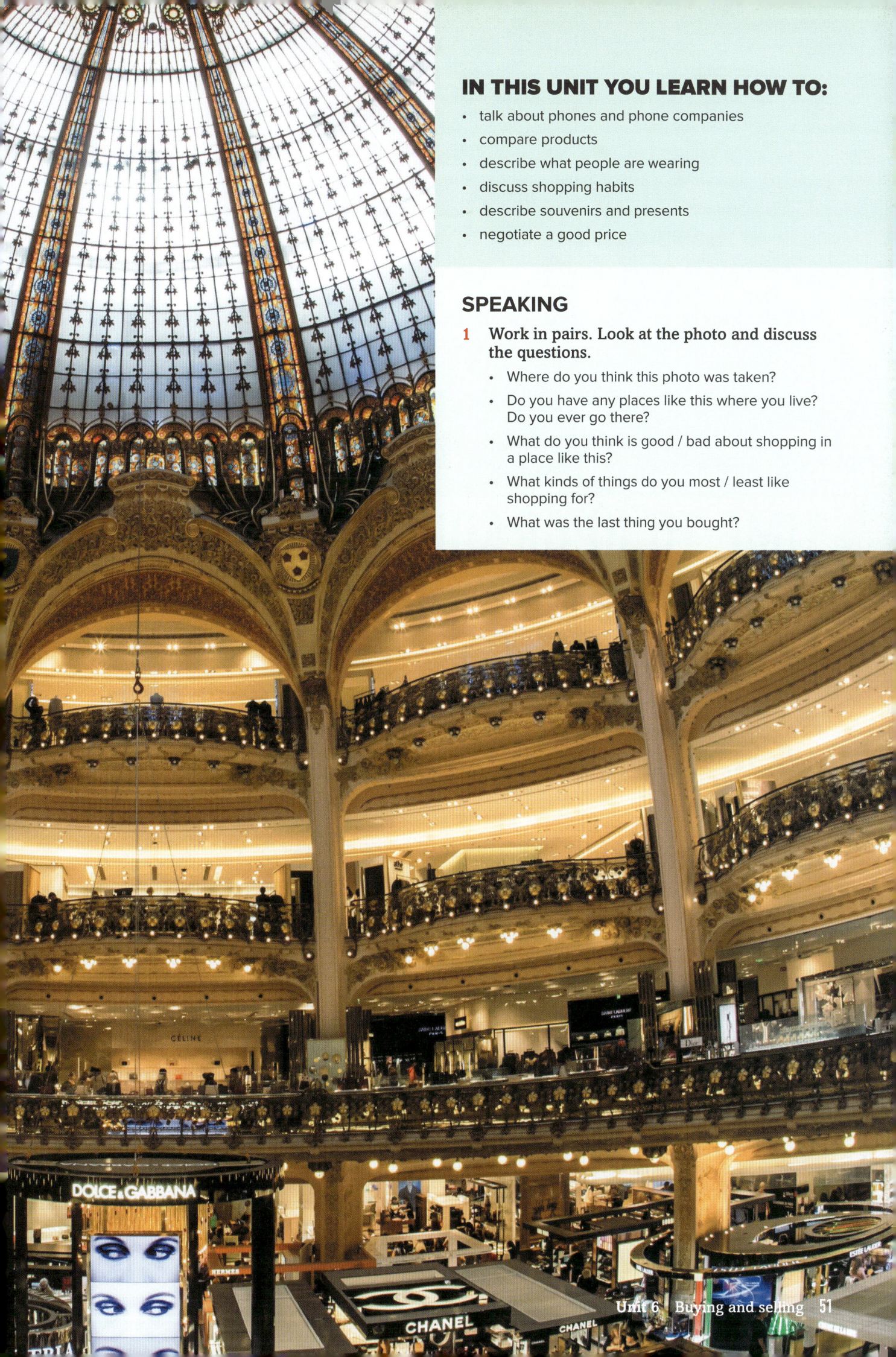

TIME TO UPGRADE

VOCABULARY Smartphones

1 Complete the sentences with the correct form of these verbs.

| charge | navigate | sign | swipe | tap |
| last | offer | store | take | upgrade |

1 My phone's out of date. **I really want to _____ to the latest version**. Its operating system is better.
2 It's not a bad phone, but **the battery only _____ a few hours**.
3 The camera on it is amazing. **It _____ great high quality pictures**.
4 It uses a touch ID system, so you don't need a password. **You just _____ your finger across the screen to unlock it**.
5 They persuaded me to _____ **a two-year contract**, but I really want to get out of it now.
6 **Can I plug my phone in here?** I need to _____ it. The battery's almost dead.
7 **If you want to turn the voice recognition on**, you just _____ this icon here.
8 The screen is beautifully designed. **It's really easy to _____ your way round**.
9 **It can _____ up to 50 voicemails** at a time.
10 **I'm with Vodafone** at the moment, but if another company could _____ a better deal, I'd switch.

2 Look at the chunks in bold in Exercise 1. Work in pairs and think of three ways each chunk could be changed.

1 I really want to upgrade to the latest version.

   I **should** upgrade to the latest version.

   I really want to upgrade to the **ePhone5**.

   I'd like to upgrade to **business class**.

3 Work with a new partner. Discuss the questions.
- How often do you upgrade?
- How long does your battery usually last?
- Do you use the camera on your phone much? What do you take photos of most?
- Who are you with? Why did you choose that company?
- What kind of deal do you have?

LISTENING

4 ▶ 29 Listen to a conversation in a mobile phone shop. Complete the table about the two different phones discussed. Then work in pairs and compare your answers.

	S620	N570
Monthly payments		
Screen	fairly small	
Battery life		
Camera (megapixels)		
Storage capacity		
Speakers	fairly small	
Number of minutes / texts per month *first* offered		

5 What was the final deal the customer was offered? Would you accept this offer? Why? / Why not?

52

GRAMMAR

Comparisons

When we want to compare two things, we use a number of different patterns with adjectives or nouns. We can also modify comparatives with words like *far* and *slightly* to show how big the difference is.

6 Look at these sentences from the conversation. Answer the questions below.

   a The camera is **much more powerful**.
   b It's **a bit easier** to navigate.
   c The other phone uses a polymer battery, which **isn't as good**.
   d The screen folds out, so it's **about twice the size of** your current phone's.
   e It's **about twice as big as** the speaker you currently have.

   1 Why does the comparative adjective in a) use *more*, but the comparative in b) doesn't?
   2 Which word used before the adjective shows a big difference?
   3 Which phrase used before the adjective shows a small difference?
   4 Do you know any other words that show how big / small a difference is?
   5 Which sentence is a negative comparison? Which structure is used?
   6 How are the structures in bold in d) and e) different from each other? Why?

G Check your ideas on page 93 and do Exercise 1.

7 ▶ 29 The words in italics in these sentences about the two phones are factually incorrect. Correct them, then listen again and check your answers.

   1 The N570 offers a *slightly* better user experience.
   2 The N570 *isn't as easy* to navigate *as* the S620.
   3 The lithium-ion battery lasts *a tiny bit* longer than the other one.
   4 The camera on the N570 is *almost* twice as powerful.
   5 The S620 can store far *more* photos than the N570.
   6 The speaker on the N570 is *a bit smaller*.

8 Make the sentences below true for you by choosing the best words in italics. Then work in pairs and share your ideas. Explain as much as you can about each one.

   1 I'm *less / slightly more / much more* interested in technology than I was five years ago.
   2 Sending texts is *not as easy as / far easier than / a bit easier than* calling someone.
   3 Using mobiles while driving is *a lot more dangerous than / a bit more dangerous than / as dangerous as / not as dangerous as* drink driving.
   4 I feel *far safer / a tiny bit safer / less safe* when I have my mobile phone with me.
   5 For me, when it comes to choosing a phone, battery life is *a lot more important than / a tiny bit more important than / not as important as* the brand.
   6 Now so many people have smartphones, the quality of life is *way better / quite a lot better / slightly better / a bit worse* than it was in the past.

G For further practice, see Exercise 2 on page 93.

DEVELOPING CONVERSATIONS

Avoiding repetition

To talk about the differences between things, we often use *one / ones* to avoid repeating the noun. To join contrasting parts of the sentences together, we often use *whereas / while*.

And then the camera is much more powerful. This **one** is 32 megapixels, **whereas** the **one** on the S620 is just 15.

9 Match the two parts of the sentences.

   1 This phone comes with a nice protective cover,
   2 This one only has 100 megabytes of memory,
   3 This one is only £43.99,
   4 These phones are on special offer,
   5 These ones all use a touch ID system,
   6 You can store up to 500 messages on this one,

   a whereas this one is £85.
   b whereas this one has 250.
   c whereas this one doesn't.
   d while that one only has room for 250.
   e while those just use a password, which isn't as secure.
   f while those ones aren't.

10 Work in groups. Compare the features of any phones you have. Find at least three ways in which each one is different from the others. Use *one / ones* and *whereas / while*.

CONVERSATION PRACTICE

11 Work in pairs. You are going to roleplay a conversation in a mobile phone shop.

   Student A: you are a customer. Read File 4 on page 98.

   Student B: you are a salesperson. Read File 8 on page 99.

12 Now roleplay the conversation. Use as much language from this lesson as you can.

10 To watch the video and do the activities, see the DVD ROM.

Unit 6 Buying and selling 53

SHOP TILL YOU DROP

VOCABULARY Clothes and accessories

1 Work in pairs. Tell each other as much as you can about the clothes and accessories you are wearing at the moment. Think about:
   - why you chose them.
   - where you got them.
   - how long you've had them.

2 With your partner, decide which is the odd one out in each group. Explain your decisions.
   1 necklace / bracelet / chain / belt / ring
   2 top / shirt / jacket / skirt / jumper
   3 jeans / trousers / earrings / tracksuit bottoms / leggings
   4 slippers / trainers / sandals / boots / high heels
   5 scarf / gloves / T-shirt / wool hat / thick socks
   6 scruffy / trendy / smart / cool / nice
   7 colourful / stripy / tight / bright / plain / checked

3 How many of the things in Exercise 2 can you see in your classroom? Which do you like best? Why?

4 Work in pairs. Say what you think of the way the people in the photos are dressed. Use some of the language from Exercise 2 and the phrases below.

   - That top / shirt doesn't fit him / her properly.
   - Those trainers / socks (don't) really suit him / her.
   - Those trainers (don't) really match / (don't) really go with that / those ...

READING

5 Read the questionnaire opposite about attitudes to shopping, fashion and money. Circle the answers that are most true for you. Then work in pairs. Compare your answers and explain your choices.

6 With your partner, look at File 9 on page 99. Calculate your scores and read the descriptions. Is the description of you accurate? Why? / Why not?

7 Match the definitions below to the words in italics in the questionnaire.
   1 something that doesn't follow – or that breaks – a rule
   2 a set of clothes that you wear together
   3 buying things in order to make yourself feel happy
   4 something far more expensive than it should be
   5 without getting what you wanted
   6 old but valuable because it's in great condition and it's rare or unusual
   7 in a situation where you owe money
   8 unattractive and bad quality

8 Work in pairs. Invent a very short story using six of the words in Exercise 7. Then tell it to another pair.

SPEAKING

9 Work in groups. Discuss the questions.
   - How much pressure do you think there is on young people to have expensive products and designer brands? Where does the pressure come from? Do you worry about it at all? Why? / Why not?
   - Is debt an issue in your country? Why?
   - Do you ever check where / how the things you buy were produced?
   - Do you buy much online? Is online shopping having an effect on shops in your country? How?
   - Can you think of any shops that have had bad publicity because of the way they make / get their products – or the way they run their business? What happened?

Shop till you drop!

1 How keen on shopping are you?
a Not at all. I find it boring and often stressful. I avoid it if I can.
b It's OK if you go with friends, or have nothing else to do.
c Very. I go all the time. I love it.

2 What's the most important thing when you buy clothes?
a They're cheap.
b They will last a long time.
c They look good on me.

3 If you see something you really like, but can't really afford, what do you do?
a I just do without it. I don't really need it anyway.
b I save up and buy it when I have enough money or when it's in the sales.
c I buy it with a credit card. I don't mind being *in debt* for a week or two.

4 If you go shopping and come back *empty-handed*, how do you feel?
a A bit frustrated, but I like to shop around for the best bargains and sometimes it takes time.
b I don't mind. Sometimes it's nice just to go window-shopping.
c I never come back empty-handed! What's the point of going shopping if you don't buy anything?

5 Have you ever lied to someone about the price of something?
a Yes. I didn't want them to realise how little I'd spent.
b No, never. Why should I?
c Yes. I didn't want them to realise how much I'd spent.

6 When you include trainers, boots and sandals, how many pairs of shoes do you own?
a 5 pairs or fewer.
b 6–19 pairs.
c I've lost count. It must be at least 20.

7 Do you have any clothes you only wear at home?
a Yes, they have holes in, but they're OK to wear around the house.
b Yes. They're not fashionable, but they're comfortable.
c No. You never know who will call at your house. I always look my best.

8 Do you have any clothing you haven't worn much?
a Not really, but I have one *outfit* I only wear on special occasions.
b Yes. It doesn't fit me at the moment, but it will once I lose some weight!
c Yes. One piece still has the price tag on.

9 Are there any shops you normally avoid going to?
a Yes, because I don't like the politics connected with the shop.
b No, not really. I sometimes worry about how things were made, but I also love a bargain!
c Not really. I don't really like shops full of cheap, *nasty* clothes, but they're still worth looking in.

10 Do you ever buy designer brands?
a Never. They're *a rip-off*. You're just paying for the label.
b Sometimes – especially if they are in the sales.
c All the time. Designer brands are just better.

11 Do you believe in *retail therapy*?
a Not at all. Buying things doesn't make you happy.
b Shopping isn't the first thing I think of to cheer myself up, but it does work sometimes.
c Absolutely. If I'm feeling down, going shopping or buying something always cheers me up.

12 Have you ever had to buy an extra bag to bring home all the purchases you made on holiday?
a Never. Holidays are supposed to be relaxing and the last thing I want to do is go shopping.
b Once I did, but it was *an exception*.
c I usually make sure I have plenty of space in my luggage before I go because I know I'll do loads of shopping.

13 Do you ever buy second-hand clothes?
a Only if they fit me OK and they're really cheap!
b No. I can't stand the idea of wearing something that someone else wore before me!
c Of course! You can find some incredible *vintage* clothes in second-hand shops.

14 How often do you look at fashion magazines?
a Never. They are stupid. A complete waste of time.
b Sometimes. If they are in a waiting room or someone else has bought them, I like to have a look.
c I regularly buy them.

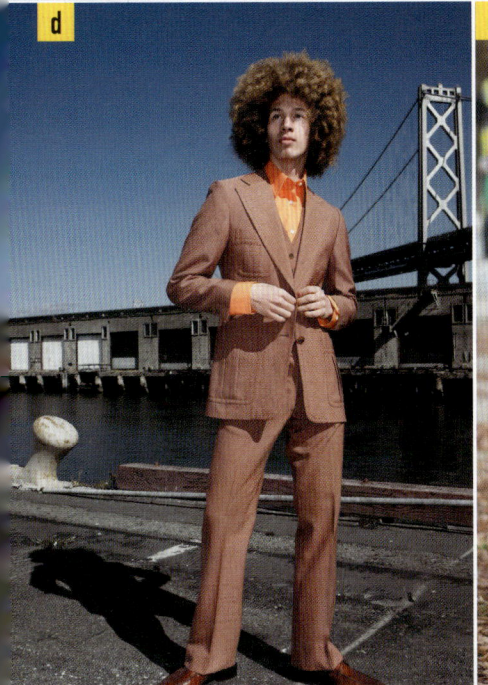

Unit 6 Buying and selling

SOUVENIR SHOP

SPEAKING

1 Work in pairs. Look at the photos and discuss the questions.
   - What part of the world do you think each of the souvenirs is from?
   - How much would you pay for each of these things? Why?
   - How would you put the souvenirs in order from the best to the worst?

VOCABULARY Describing souvenirs and presents

2 Put the words in the box into three groups:
   1 material
   2 how things are produced
   3 object

carved	leather	printed	silk	woven
clay	magnet	plastic	mask	straw
doll	pot	wood	glass	model
wool	handmade	rug	painted	scarf

3 Work in pairs. Describe the things in the photos using words from Exercise 2.

4 Work with a new partner. What objects do you have that are made of the materials in Exercise 2? Tell your partner about them.

LISTENING

5 ▶ 30 Listen to four people talking about gifts and souvenirs. Match each speaker (1–4) to one of the following. There are two you do not need. Which person:
   a threw away the gift?
   b collects magnets to put on their fridge?
   c wasn't pleased with a gift?
   d was given a useful souvenir?
   e prefers food or drink as souvenirs?
   f talks about a souvenir breaking?

6 ▶ 30 Work in pairs. Discuss which speakers had these souvenirs, where each souvenir was from and how the speakers described them. Listen again and check your ideas.

an apron	a model	a paperweight
a drink	pannetone	a tie

7 Work in groups. Discuss the questions.
- What are typical souvenirs from your country?
- Do you agree that the best souvenirs are things you can consume? Why? / Why not?
- Do you think the designer is being ungrateful not wanting the gifts?
- What's the most useful souvenir you've bought or been given?
- Have you ever got upset about breaking something? What was it? What happened?

GRAMMAR

Noun phrases
We often add information before and after a noun to help describe it. This longer group of words is called a noun phrase.

8 Look at how some nouns from the listening are added to. Then work in pairs and decide if the statements below are true.

a *The **student** bought me a **tie**.*
b ***My wife's student** bought me a **tie**.*
c *My wife's student bought me a **silk tie**.*
d *My wife's student bought me a **horrible** silk **tie**.*
e *My wife's student bought me a horrible **bright** silk **tie**.*
f *My wife's student bought me a horrible bright silk **tie** **with a picture**.*
g *My wife's student bought me a horrible bright silk tie with a **picture of the Great Wall** on it.*

1 The compound noun *silk tie* describes a kind of silk – NOT a kind of tie.
2 Both nouns in the compound noun *silk tie* can be made plural (i.e. *silks ties*).
3 We use 's to talk about a particular person or thing belonging to or connected to a particular person, animal or organisation.
4 The general rule for the order of adjectives is opinion first and then facts such as size or colour.
5 We can add information after the noun using phrases that start with different prepositions (e.g. *with*, *of*, *from*, *in*, etc.).

G Check your ideas on page 93 and do Exercise 1.

9 Put the words in brackets into the correct order before the nouns. Add correct prepositions after the nouns where necessary.

1 My favourite piece of clothing is a _____ hat _____ Peru that my dad bought for me. (lovely / wool)
2 My most precious possession is my _____ ring. (gold / grandmother's / old)
3 People there often cook in _____ pots _____ a top like a kind of chimney. (clay / wonderful)
4 I recently bought this _____ coat _____ the winter. (leather / nice / brown)

5 My flatmates think I'm a bit weird because I keep a _____ bear _____ my bed, but I don't care. It means a lot to me. (teddy / cute / yellow)
6 When I was on holiday in Tanzania, I bought this _____ mask _____ a devil. It's on my wall at home. (hand-carved / wood / amazing)

10 Complete the sentences with your own ideas. Use a noun phrase. Then work in groups and share your ideas.

1 My favourite piece of clothing is ...
2 When I was on holiday in ... I bought ...
3 My most precious possession is ...

G For further practice, see Exercise 2 on page 94.

DEVELOPING CONVERSATIONS

Negotiating prices
When you buy souvenirs and other things, you may need to negotiate a price. Seller and buyers often use common phrases to justify the price they offer.

11 ▶ 31 Decide if a seller or a buyer would say these phrases. Then listen to a negotiation about a leather jacket and check your ideas.

1 That's very expensive.
2 It's top quality.
3 It's genuine.
4 It'll last forever.
5 I won't make any money like that.
6 I've seen similar ones that are cheaper.
7 I don't have much money left.
8 Take it or leave it. I can't go lower than that.

12 Write three more things either the buyer or seller might say to justify their price.

PRONUNCIATION

13 ▶ 32 Listen to some pairs of numbers and notice the change in intonation when we express surprise. Then listen again and repeat.

14 Work in pairs. Look at Track 31 on page 111 and decide who will take which role. Read out the conversation, using intonation to express surprise where necessary. Then change roles and repeat.

SPEAKING

15 Work in pairs.

Student A: you are a tourist thinking of buying one of the things in the photos in this lesson.

Student B: you are the seller.

Negotiate the price.

Unit 6 Buying and selling 57

VIDEO 3

WHEELIN' AND DEALIN' ANTIQUES

1 Work in pairs and look at the photo. What kind of place do you think it is? What are the people selling?

2 Check you understand the words in bold below. Which of the following is good advice for selling in a place like this? Why? / Why not?
   1 Don't try to sell things that are broken or **'garbage'**.
   2 Be quite **aggressive** and decisive when negotiating.
   3 Don't worry about having a **display** that is very organised or **disciplined**.
   4 Make sure you have a price **tag** on everything.
   5 Put the most expensive things at the front of the **stall**.
   6 Always give a price that is higher than you think it's worth.

3 ▶ 11 Watch a reality TV show where two men are selling things in a flea market to raise money with the help of an expert. Complete the table for the two men.

	Steve (man in white T-shirt)	Trent (man with cowboy hat)
Raising money to ...	1_____	–
Best sale	$2_____ for 3_____	$4_____ for 5_____
Fails to sell	a trunk	6_____ white chairs Apollo 11 toy
Good salesman	negotiates well	good 7_____ – organised and disciplined
Bad salesman	8_____	not decisive enough shouldn't put 9_____ on

4 ▶ 11 Work in pairs. Which of the things in Exercise 3 does the word *it* refer to in each sentence? Watch again to check your ideas.
   1 Someone ... turned **it** into a target and just started shooting at **it** ...
   2 ... there's some stickers that have an 'O' and a 'K' on them throughout the frame. Erm, I had four on **it**. I would probably take three on **it**.
   3 ... everything is set up right. **It**'s organised. **It**'s disciplined.
   4 I like the colour. I like the beat-up look. I think **it** was a fair deal.
   5 ... if you came here like an hour ago, **it** was empty or nothing sitting on top of **it** ...

5 Work in groups. Discuss the questions.
   • Are there any similar markets where you live?
   • Do you like looking round these kinds of markets? Why? / Why not?
   • Would you be any good at selling in a flea market?
   • What reality shows like this do you have on TV? Do you watch any? Why? / Why not?

UNDERSTANDING FAST SPEECH

6 ▶ 12 Read and listen to this extract from the video said at natural pace and then slowed down. To help you, groups of words are marked with / and pauses are marked //. Stressed sounds are in CAPITALS.

I've ACtually seen OTHer things that are THIS / BUllet / SCULPted // KIND of appeal / and its JUST inCREdible that this / GOssamer OBject / HOlds toGEther AFter having been abUSed / for // you know / HUNdreds of YEARS // with BUllets shot through it / so // it's GREAT

7 Now you have a go! Practise saying the extract at natural pace.

58

REVIEW 3

GRAMMAR

1 Complete the dialogue with one word in each space. Contractions count as one word.

A: What do you do?
B: I work ¹_____ a construction company.
A: Oh yeah, ²_____ what?
B: I'm an electrician.
A: Really? I thought most electricians are self-employed.
B: Yeah, they are. I mean I was, but with this job my hours are a ³_____ more regular. I ⁴_____ have to work weekends very often. Obviously, the money isn't ⁵_____ good. But I don't mind that.
A: So do you do any private work?
B: We're not ⁶_____ to, but I do occasionally – for people I know, usually.
A: So it ⁷_____ be a big company you work for.
B: Yeah, it ⁸_____. It's huge. They're involved ⁹_____ all sorts of projects here and abroad, so I get to travel a bit.
A: You ¹⁰_____ enjoy that.
B: I ¹¹_____ sometimes, but it depends where it is and if I ¹²_____ get back home for the weekend.

2 Complete the second sentence so that it has a similar meaning to the first sentence using the word given. Do not change the word given. You must use between three and five words, including the word given.

1. The company dress code doesn't allow jeans.
   We _____ at work. **CAN'T**
2. When we go to the toilet we mustn't leave our desks for more than five minutes.
   We _____ a toilet break of more than five minutes. **ALLOWED**
3. I really shouldn't leave before six, but I could maybe go at five.
   I'm _____ until six, but I could maybe go at five. **STAY**
4. On this one, the design's nicer but the battery life is shorter than on that one.
   On this one, the design's nicer but the battery doesn't _____ on the other one. **LAST**
5. Paris has around ten million people, compared with about twenty million in Mexico City.
   Mexico city is _____ Paris. **SIZE**

3 Complete the sentences by putting the words in brackets in the correct order.

1. He bought me a _____ (nice / really / scarf / wool) yesterday.
2. They sell a lot of _____ (Big Ben / tacky / of / plastic / models).
3. She was wearing a _____ ('Peace' / blue / with / T-shirt / scruffy / written) on it.
4. I like the leather jacket, but I've seen _____ (that / ones / far / cheaper / similar / are).
5. His favourite piece of clothing is _____ (a / shirt / name / Barcelona / classic / with / Messi's) on it.

4 ▶ 33 Listen and write the six sentences you hear.

VOCABULARY

5 Match the verbs (1–8) with the collocates (a–h).

1 take   a to chemicals / to huge risks
2 ignore   b 500 voicemails / up to 32GB
3 introduce   c my phone / to the latest version
4 sign   d a lot of abuse / used to it
5 store   e the rules / health and safety
6 upgrade   f a new rule / an offer for customers
7 be exposed   g them to court / it or leave it
8 get   h a six-year contract / below

6 Decide if these words are connected to work, phones or clothes.

admin	icon	gloves	tap
plug	rewarding	thick	bonus
plain	swipe	demanding	tight

7 Complete the sentences. Use the word in brackets to form a word that fits in the space.

1. There's a legal _____ to give workers two weeks' holiday pay. (require)
2. The government doesn't do enough to enforce the _____ laws. (employ)
3. There's still a lot of _____ against women in the workplace. (discriminate)
4. I could never be a security guard in a museum. I'd die of _____. (bore)
5. Being a waiter isn't a great job but it's _____ well-paid when you include the tips. (relative)
6. My main _____ is to make sure everyone gets paid on time. (responsible)
7. We got this beautiful _____ painting on holiday. It really brightens up the room. (colour)
8. I bought this amazing mask _____ from wood. (carve)
9. I normally don't let my kids buy what they want, but I made an _____ this time. (except)
10. I got into this field when it was still new, but it's far more _____ these days. (compete)

8 Complete the text with one word in each space. The first letters are given.

I'm a regional manager for a supermarket chain and I'm in ¹ch_____ of around 200 stores. It can be very ²st_____ as we are under ³pr_____ to improve sales year on year, but generally I love it because it's very ⁴va_____ – I travel and speak to lots of different people.

I'm quite unusual in that I left school when I was sixteen. I worked as a ⁵la_____ on building sites for a couple of years but I only had temporary work so it was very ⁶in_____. So then I got a job in one of the supermarket's ⁷wa_____. It was still quite hard but at least I had a permanent ⁸co_____. After a while I started ⁹ma_____ a small team. I always thought I could do ¹⁰be_____ for myself, so I ¹¹ap_____ for the company's management training scheme and they ¹²of_____ me a place. It's taken me twenty years to get to my current position.

Review 3 59

7

EDUCATION

IN THIS UNIT YOU LEARN HOW TO:

- describe courses, schools, teachers and students
- show you believe or sympathise with what people tell you
- talk about possible future plans or situations
- discuss different aspects of education
- form and say different words from the same root

SPEAKING

1 Work in groups. Look at the photo of an old Canadian schoolroom and discuss the questions.

- Why do you think these things are there?
  - the painting above the teacher
  - the piano
  - the pointed hat by the desk
  - the bell on the teacher's desk
  - the books on the teacher's desk
- Are there any similarities between this classroom and classrooms you've studied in?
- How has education changed over recent years?
- Do you think these changes have been for the better or for the worse? Why?

Unit 7   Education   61

HOW'S YOUR COURSE GOING?

VOCABULARY Describing courses

1 Match the questions (1–8) with the answers (a–h). Check you understand the words and phrases in bold.

1 Why are you doing it?
2 How's it going?
3 How was it taught?
4 Did you enjoy it?
5 What were the **tutors** like?
6 Did you have much **coursework**?
7 Did you find it useful?
8 How is it **assessed**?

a 25% of **the overall mark** is on the **coursework** and the rest is on the **final exam**.
b They've introduced a new system at work so we're all **getting training in** how to use it.
c I'm **struggling** a bit, to be honest. I failed my last **module** so I can't afford to fail another.
d Yes and no. I guess it was **good for my CV**, but it wasn't **relevant** to my current work as I never use Excel.
e They were very **encouraging** and gave us a lot of **feedback**.
f It was all done through **workshops**, so it was all very **practical**.
g Well, I started out quite **keen**, but I lost a bit of **motivation** as I wasn't making much **progress**.
h Yeah, it was quite **demanding**. We had regular **assignments** and the **seminars** involved a lot of reading beforehand too.

2 Work in pairs and answer the questions. Use a dictionary to help you if you need to.

1 What might you do for an assignment? Apart from *have*, what other verbs can go with *assignment*?
2 Why might you struggle on a course? What's the opposite of struggling on a course?
3 If tutors are encouraging, what do they say to you? Think of two more adjectives to describe a tutor.
4 When do you get feedback? Why do tutors give you feedback?
5 Think of three ways you can be assessed.
6 Think of four things you might get training in at work.
7 What things might help you maintain or increase your motivation on a course?

3 With your partner, look at these different types of courses and training. Tell your partner about any that you have done. Ask each other questions like those in Exercise 1.

a degree course	IT training
a postgraduate course	first-aid training
an evening course	leadership training
an online course	training in using a machine

LISTENING

4 ▶ 34 Listen to two colleagues on a break at work. They talk about a course the woman is doing. Take notes about the following:

1 type of course
2 how they learn
3 tutors and students
4 length of course
5 assessment & qualification

5 Do you think the course will be good for her career or not? Why? / Why not?

6 ▶ 34 Listen again and complete the sentences with three words in each space.

1 Well, you learn _____ . You know, how to listen and guide people through problems.
2 It's very practical. I mean, we have some _____ which are about theory ...
3 Great. They're all very _____ , but they present things in a very clear way.
4 Well, there are one or two guys that aren't as supportive _____ .
5 I can imagine. You want _____ !
6 I think there are eleven weeks left. It's _____ – an evening a week.
7 ... you could do more, but I don't have time _____ my workload here.

7 Work in pairs. Discuss the questions.
- Is encouragement always better than criticism?
- Do you think you would be good at counselling?
- Do you know anyone who has studied something that they don't use anymore?
- When do you think is a good time to stop studying?

GRAMMAR

Future time clauses
When we want to specify the time at which a future action will happen, we often use a clause starting with a time expression such as *when*, *after*, *once*, etc.

8 Look at these sentences from the conversation. Answer the questions below.
a *I'm going back after I've had this coffee.*
b *So what are you going to do when it ends?*
c *I might do another course once I've finished this one.*
d *As soon as I find a proper job, I'll probably stop doing any studying.*

1 What are the time expressions in each sentence?
2 Do you know any other time words like *when* and *after* that can join two parts of a sentence?
3 What tenses follow the time expressions?
4 Do the time clauses refer to now or the future?
5 Can the sentences start with the time clause?

> Check your ideas on page 94 and do Exercise 1.

9 Complete the questions with your own ideas. Then work in groups and take turns asking and answering your questions.
1 What are you going to do after ...?
2 Where are you going to stay when ...?
3 While you're on holiday ...?
4 What'll happen once ...?
5 How long is it before ...?

> For further practice, see Exercise 2 on page 95.

DEVELOPING CONVERSATIONS

I can imagine, *I bet*, etc.
When someone makes a statement about how they feel or how a situation is, you can show you believe them or sympathise with them by saying *I'm sure*, *It sounds it*, *I can imagine* or *I bet*.

P: *They can be a bit more critical than the others, which is a bit annoying.*
D: ***I can imagine.***

10 Look at Track 34 on page 111 and find examples of the phrases in the box. What feelings or situations does Daniel show he believes?

11 Complete the sentences about courses with your own ideas. Then work in pairs. Take turns reading your sentences and responding with *I bet*, etc.

A: *We have to do a huge amount of reading at home every week so I'm struggling.*
B: *I bet. It must be hard.*

1 _____ so I'm struggling.
2 _____ , which was annoying.
3 _____ so I'm really pleased.
4 _____ , which is really helpful.
5 _____ , so it's quite demanding.
6 _____ , which is a pain.

CONVERSATION PRACTICE

12 Work in pairs. You are going to roleplay a conversation between two people who are doing degrees. Either use your own ideas or choose a roleplay card (Student A: File 5, page 98; Student B: File 10, page 100). Spend a few minutes deciding what you will say. Think about how to answer the questions below.

- What are you studying?
- And what does that involve?
- Why are you doing that?
- How's it going? Are you enjoying it?
- What are your tutors like?
- And what about the other people on the course?
- Do you have much coursework?
- How's it assessed?
- How long does the course last? When does it finish?
- And what are you going to do once it ends?

13 Now roleplay the conversation. Ask and answer the questions above. Use as much language from this lesson as you can.

> 13 To watch the video and do the activities, see the DVD ROM.

Unit 7 Education 63

PAY ATTENTION

SPEAKING

1 Work in pairs. Look at the photo of a teacher and student and discuss the questions.

- Do you like the photo? Why? / Why not?
- What do you think it says about teachers and students?
- Look at these qualities connected to teachers. Are there any you would add? Are any of them not necessary to be a good teacher? What's the most important?

patient	well-prepared
friendly	strict
encouraging	knows their subject well

- Look at these qualities connected to students. Are there any you would add? Are any of them not necessary to be a good student? What's the most important?

bright	pays attention in class
enthusiastic	ambitious
does homework	a keen reader

VOCABULARY Education

2 Complete the sentences below with these words. Then work in pairs and decide if each sentence refers to a school or a university.

academic reputation	school fees
research facilities	alternative approaches
entry requirements	social problems
bilingual school	Master's programme
strict discipline	

1 It's a _____ , so some subjects like PE and science are taught in English.
2 It's very traditional. Pupils wear uniforms and there's very _____ .
3 It has a big _____ that attracts a lot of international students.
4 It has a very good _____ . They really push pupils to achieve high marks.
5 It's difficult to get into because the _____ are very high, especially for Medicine.
6 It's in quite a rough area, so they have to deal with quite a few _____ .
7 Lectures are very crowded, and _____ are a bit limited.
8 They have some _____ to teaching and learning, which the headteacher introduced.
9 The _____ are so high that only wealthy families can afford to send their kids there.

3 With your partner, think of a word or phrase connected to each of the words in the box in Exercise 2. Use a dictionary to help you.

academic reputation – top university / hard to get into

4 Work in groups. Discuss the questions.

- How many of the sentences in Exercise 2 can you use to describe schools and universities you know or have heard of?
- What places have you studied at? What were they like?

LISTENING

5 ▶ 35 Listen to four conversations about different aspects of education. Who is the main speaker in each conversation (1–4)? There is one person you do not need.

a a parent
b a school teacher
c a university lecturer
d an overseas student
e a postgraduate student

6 ▶ 35 Work in pairs and answer the questions. Then listen again and check your answers.

1 Why is the teacher annoyed? What advice is he given?
2 Why is the overseas student unhappy? What is she going to do?
3 What rule does the lecturer explain? Are there any exceptions to the rule?
4 Why is the parent happy?

7 With your partner, try to remember which verbs went with these nouns in the four conversations. Then look at Track 35 on page 111 and compare your ideas.

1 _____ attention, _____ to each other, _____ their respect
2 _____ one of the questions, _____ my score, _____ the test
3 _____ a deadline, _____ an exception, _____ any excuses
4 _____ the kids, _____ classes, _____ a good reputation

8 Work in pairs. Discuss the questions.
- What do you think the teacher in the first conversation should do? Why?
- How were difficult students dealt with in your school? Do you think it was a good approach?
- Have you ever made a stupid mistake in an exam / a test? If yes, what did you do?
- Do you know anyone who has changed schools? Why?

GRAMMAR

Zero and first conditionals

We use conditional sentences to talk about situations and their results. In zero and first conditionals, we use present tenses in the *if*-clause to talk about general, present and possible future situations.

9 Look at these sentences from the conversations. Then work in pairs and answer the questions below.

a If I **try** to explain something, they **sit** whispering to each other.
b If they **talk**, **send** them to the headteacher.
c If they **don't accept** me, I**'ll** either **retake** the test or I **might look** for another Master's.
d If you **have** any problems which are affecting your coursework, you **should contact** the student counselling service.

1 Which sentence is about a situation that has already happened before and may happen again?
2 Which sentences show possible future situations? What tense is used in the *if*-clause?
3 What's the difference in meaning between *will* and *might*?
4 Which two clauses give advice about possible future situations?

G Check your ideas on page 95 and do Exercise 1.

In conversations, we often ask *What (happens) if …?* When we answer these questions, we don't usually repeat the *if*-clause. We generally only say the result clause.

A: *If you miss a deadline that your tutor has set, you will be given a zero.*
B: *… but what if you have a family crisis or something?*
A: *Well, obviously we'll make an exception for certain cases.*

10 Complete the sentences with the correct form of the verbs.

A: What are you going to do when you graduate?
B: It depends on my marks. If I ¹_____ a good degree, I ²_____ a Master's in Business Administration. (get, probably / do)
A: And what if you don't?
B: I'm not sure. I ³_____ travelling for a while if I ⁴_____ in too much debt. (go, not / be)
C: What happens if I lose the key for my room?
D: ⁵_____ the security guard to open it. (ask)
C: And what if he ⁶_____ at the front desk? (not / be)
D: ⁷_____ around. Just ⁸_____ the emergency number. Someone from the main office ⁹_____ . (not / wait, call, come)

11 Write answers to these questions.
1 What are you going to do in the summer holidays?
2 What happens if I'm struggling in class?
3 How do you think your life will change in the next few years?

12 Work in pairs. Take turns asking the questions in Exercise 11. Say the reply you wrote. Your partner should continue the conversation by asking *And what if …?* How long can you continue each conversation?

G For further practice, see Exercise 2 on page 95.

SPEAKING

13 Work in groups. Look at the rules below connected to education from round the world. Discuss the questions.
- Do you have any of these rules – or similar ones – in your country?
- Which rules do you think are good and which do you think are bad? Why?
- Why do you think these rules were introduced?
- What results might these rules cause?
- Do you think any of these rules should be introduced (or reversed) in your country? Why?

IN THE UK, if a child skips school, the parents can be fined.

IN ITALY, if you fail three or more subjects, you have to repeat the whole year.

IN SOME STATES IN THE USA, teachers get increased pay if their students get good exam grades.

IN CHINA, you can't graduate (whatever the degree) unless you pass an English test.

IN CANADA, in some academic jobs you can't ever be fired unless you break a law.

Unit 7 Education

MAKING A DIFFERENCE

READING

1 Work in groups. What do you think the following people worry or complain about when discussing schools and the education system?

| parents | teachers | students |
| politicians | business people | |

2 Compare your ideas as a class. What do you think is the biggest education issue in your country at the moment? What solutions have been suggested? Do you agree with them?

3 Read a short article about the academic John Hattie, author of *Visible Learning*, and his research into achievement in schools. Find out:
   1 if any of the worries or issues you thought of were investigated.
   2 why the following figures are mentioned: 15, 60,000, 250 million.
   3 what Hattie believes are the most important factors.
   4 why his work is called *Visible Learning*.

4 Work in groups of three. Below are nine factors Hattie studied that the article goes on to discuss. What do you think are the top two most effective factors and what are the bottom two?
   a Teachers having high levels of subject knowledge
   b Programmes to extend students' vocabulary
   c Setting up schools outside of government control
   d Reducing class sizes by 50%
   e Providing information on how students will be assessed and feedback on what they did
   f Talking about students' expectations
   g Practising what you have learnt over time
   h Doing homework
   i Summer holidays

5 Work with the same group. You are going to read about how effective the nine factors in Exercise 4 are.

   Student A: read File 6 on page 98.

   Student B: read File 12 on page 100.

   Student C: read File 13 on page 101.

   Then work together and rank the factors from 1 (= most effective) to 9 (= least effective).

6 With your group, discuss the questions.
   • What do you think of the results of the research? Did you find anything surprising or obvious? Why?
   • How many of these factors were present in schools you have been to?
   • Do you think the results would be the same in all countries in the world? Why? / Why not?

WHAT WORKS IN EDUCATION

Few things cause more worry and debate than education. Wherever you go in the world, you will rarely find a place where everyone is happy with the education system they have. Parents worry about their kids' grades; businesses complain that students don't have the right skills; politicians look at other countries' education systems and see only failure in their own. All want to see higher achievement, but the debate is how to do it. Should it be smaller classes or more homework, wearing school uniform or better pay for teachers?

Not only are there a huge number of things that people say will make education better, but people also disagree about whether each factor actually improves learning or not. So who's right? This is the question that the New Zealand academic John Hattie tried to answer over fifteen years of work when he analysed 60,000 studies into student achievement carried out with around 250 million students, mainly from English-speaking countries around the world. It's an amazing piece of work and has produced some surprising results.

Hattie discovered that, with only very few exceptions, *every* factor which people think will improve students' achievement does work to some degree, when compared with doing nothing! He therefore quickly realised that rather than asking what policies and actions are positive, he needed to compare the size of the improvements. This resulted in a league table of over one hundred factors showing what really helps and what is less effective.

Hattie's interpretation of this table is that it is passionate teachers that make the big difference. These teachers don't have to be specialists in their field with MAs and PhDs, but they need to understand what level their students are at and show them how to exceed their expectations. In contrast, the things that often cause the loudest arguments or cost the most money – such as uniforms or reducing class sizes or investing in IT – have a relatively small impact. Hattie suggests they continue to get more attention because these are the things that parents and politicians can *see*, whereas we don't see teachers and students at work. This is why he calls his analysis *Visible Learning*: he wants to show those factors that can make a big difference.

So what are the specific factors that score best in improving performance and which ones are less effective?

UNDERSTANDING VOCABULARY

Forming words

One way to build your vocabulary is to learn the noun and the verb form of words, e.g. *achieve* and *achievement*. Common noun endings are: *-ment*, *-tion*, *-ation*, *-ance*, *-ence*, *-ist*. Many words, such as *worry*, are both nouns and verbs. Make sure you learn the pronunciation *and* collocations that go with the different forms to help you use them correctly.

7 Complete the phrases (1–8) with nouns from the article that are based on the verbs in bold.
   1 need further _____ (**improve** standards)
   2 get a good _____ in the exam (teachers **grade** the essays)
   3 a _____ in data analysis (**specialise** in marketing)
   4 a big _____ between them (the effects **differ** widely)
   5 measure students' _____ (**perform** well in the test)
   6 meet my _____ (**expect** great things of you)
   7 the project was a _____ (**fail** an exam)
   8 improve your _____ of the subject (**know** a bit of French)

PRONUNCIATION

8 ▶ 36 Listen to ten verbs and nouns with the same root and underline the main stress. Notice how the position of the main stress can change.
   1 know – knowledge   6 interpret – interpretation
   2 analyse – analysis   7 worry – worry
   3 assess – assessment   8 increase – increase
   4 define – definition   9 refund – refund
   5 inform – information   10 protest – protest

9 Practise saying the pairs of words.

10 Choose three pairs of words from Exercise 8 and write short phrases like those in Exercise 7. Then work in pairs and read out your examples.

11 Work in groups. Discuss the questions.
   - What improvements could be made in your education system? Explain why and how.
   - Do you use the knowledge you gained at school in your life much? In what ways? Is there anything you think should be taught that isn't?
   - What expectations do you have of your future life? Do you think they are high or low? Why?
   - What protests have you heard about in education? What were the people protesting about?

Unit 7 Education 67

8

IN THIS UNIT YOU LEARN HOW TO:

- describe different dishes and ways of cooking food
- explain what is on a menu
- discuss experiences of foreign food
- make generalisations
- describe restaurants

SPEAKING

1 Work in pairs. Discuss the questions.
- What do you think this man is making? Where do you think this photo was taken?
- Are you any good at cooking? If you are, how did you learn?
- What is the best dish you can cook?
- What kind of thing do you usually eat: in the morning? for lunch? in the evening?
- Are you a fussy eater, an unadventurous eater or an adventurous eater?
- Do you prefer to eat out at a restaurant or at home? Why?

EATING

I'LL GO FOR THAT

VOCABULARY Describing food

1 Label the picture with these cooking verbs.

| deep-fry | steam | mash | slice | grill |
| marinate | stir-fry | grate | boil | roast |

2 Work in groups. Discuss the questions.
- Which of the ways of cooking in Exercise 1 are most used in your house? To cook what?
- Which do you think is the easiest to do? Which is the most complicated? Why?
- Are there any ways of cooking you can't do or have never tried?

3 Work in pairs. Think of two examples of food for each of the adjectives below. Can you see any food in the picture that could be described using these adjectives?

| bland | filling | juicy | sour | tasty |
| fattening | greasy | raw | spicy | tender |

4 Work in pairs. Look at the photos in File 14 on page 101. Discuss the questions.
- Which of these things do you eat most often?
- Are there any things here you have never eaten?
- What's the best way to cook each one?
- Which could you describe using the adjectives in Exercise 3?
- Do you know anyone who can't – or doesn't – eat any of these things? Why not?

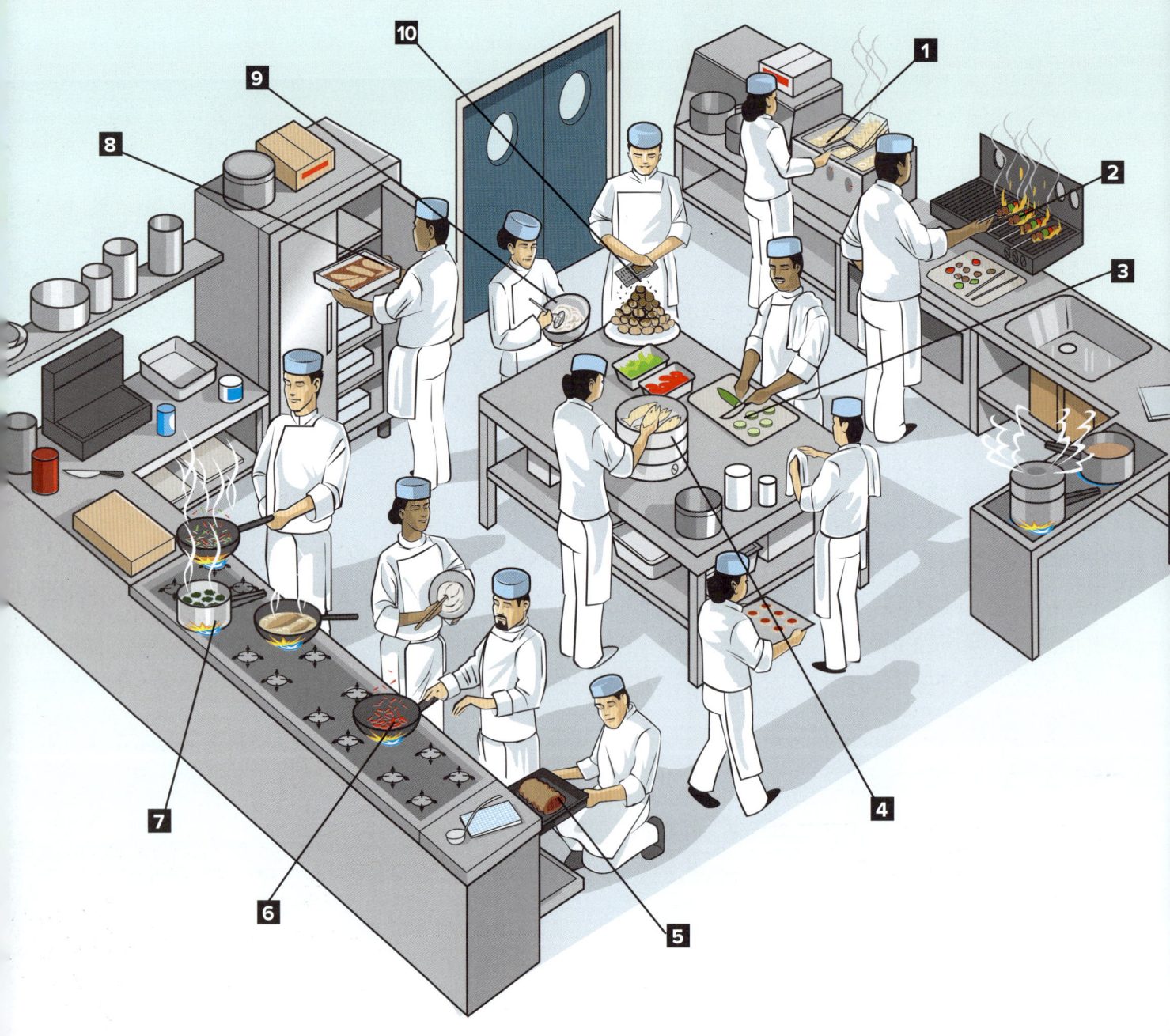

70

LISTENING

5 Look at the menu from a Peruvian restaurant. Do you know what kind of dishes they might be or what might be in them? Do any of the words sound similar to food or dishes in your language?

6 ▶ 37 Listen to a conversation between Aurora, a Peruvian businesswoman, and Claes, who is visiting Peru. Tick the dishes he decides to order and take notes on the reasons he gives for rejecting the dishes below.

1 Papa Rellena
2 Anticuchos
3 Lomo Saltado

7 ▶ 37 Listen again and complete the sentences with one word in each space.

1 They don't have an English menu, I'm _____ .
2 You'll just have to talk me _____ it.
3 That's balls of mashed potato, _____ with beef, raisins and olives.
4 It's sliced cow's heart, very _____ and _____ .
5 I'll go _____ that.
6 That's steak, sliced very _____ and then fried and _____ with rice.
7 It's a bit _____ a Spanish paella, but _____ .
8 It's a _____ of stew with goat meat in.
9 They serve it with beans on the _____ .
10 That sounds very _____ .

8 Work in pairs. Discuss the questions.
- Would you order any of the dishes mentioned? If yes, which ones? If not, why not?
- Do you like steak? If so, how do you usually like it?
- Do any of the dishes sound similar to any dishes from your country?
- Do you think your country has a national dish?
- Did they mention any ingredients you often / never use in your own cooking?

DEVELOPING CONVERSATIONS

Describing dishes
When we have to explain different foods or dishes, we often use the patterns below.

It's a kind of vegetable / side dish / spice.
It's a bit like an oyster, **but** small**er** / **but not as** big.
It's made from plums or pears / a special kind of bean.
It's cooked with tomatoes and onions and spices.

9 Think of four different kinds of drinks, dishes, fruit or vegetables from your country. Decide how to describe them using the structures above and any other useful language from this lesson.

10 Work in groups. Take turns to describe your food. Can the rest of the group guess what you are describing?

MENU

- Papa Rellena -
- Sopa de Carne -
- Anticuchos -
- Tallarín con Mariscos -
- Ceviche -
- Bistec Apanado -
- Lomo Saltado -
- Arroz con Mariscos -
- Seco de Cabrito -
- Arroz con Pato -
- Arroz con Leche -
- Helado de Lúcuma -
- Crema Volteada -
- Mazamorra Morada -

CONVERSATION PRACTICE

11 Write a typical menu for a restaurant in your country. Write it in your own language. Include two or three dishes for each stage of the meal.

12 Work in pairs. Roleplay a conversation like the one you heard in Exercise 6.

Student A: you're visiting the country on holiday or on business. You don't speak the local language.

Student B: talk Student A through the menu.

Student A: reject at least two things. Explain why. Then decide what you'd like to eat for starter, main course and dessert.

When you have finished, change roles and have another conversation.

🎥 14 To watch the video and do the activities, see the DVD ROM.

Unit 8   Eating   71

CULTURE CLASH

SPEAKING

1 Work in pairs. Read the introduction of an article about foreign food culture and living abroad below. Then discuss these questions.

- What foreign cuisines can you get in restaurants in your town / city? Do you ever eat in any of these places? If yes, what do you usually order?
- Are there many specialist shops selling foreign food where you live? Why? / Why not?
- Do you ever buy foreign / imported food? If so, what? If not, why not?
- What food from your country would you miss if you went to live abroad? Is there anything you wouldn't miss?
- Do you agree with the author's opinions?

FOOD FOR THOUGHT Look around most big cities and you'll find a wide range of restaurants serving foreign food and shops selling specialist products from abroad.

Some of them have perhaps been set up by adventurous locals trying to introduce something fresh and new. However, in most cases they were probably set up by foreigners who simply couldn't cope with the food of their host country. These places represent everything their owners miss about their home countries. Essentially they say 'I may love your people, your job opportunities, your climate, but let me show you what *real* food is!' In fact, maybe we can say that you have only fully integrated into your new country when you have accepted its food culture. So if you're living abroad, how are you finding its food culture? Are you used to it yet, or is full integration some way off?

READING

2 Work in groups of four: two As and two Bs. You are going to read the rest of the article.

Student As: read the texts on these pages.

Student Bs: read the texts in File 15 on page 102.

With the person who read the *same* texts, answer the questions.

1 Where are the two people in your texts from?
2 Where are they living now? Why?
3 What do they like about the food and the way people eat there?
4 Is there anything they miss about their home?
5 Is there anything they still find strange or annoying about the host country?
6 Is there anything they'll never get used to? Why?

3 Now work in pairs: one Student A and one Student B. Ask and answer the questions in Exercise 2 about the texts you read.

4 With the same partner, complete the sentences with words and phrases from all four texts. The definitions in brackets will help you.

1 Ian said 'stinky tofu' smells like sweaty socks and rotting fish and it's really _____ . (making you not want to eat it)
2 Ian said Americans usually just _____ the bill. (divide equally)
3 Isabella didn't like having dinner at six in the evening. She was always _____ by bedtime. (really hungry)

IAN (American)

I moved to Taiwan five years ago because my wife is from Taipei, and I love it here. We eat out a lot and there are lots of good, cheap restaurants and street snacks. I'm vegetarian and there's a long tradition of veggie food here so it's great for me. Having said that, I'll never get used to 'stinky tofu'. The name is very accurate – it smells like sweaty socks mixed with rotting fish! I tried it once. The sauce was actually OK, but that smell is just so off-putting!

When you go to restaurants here, generally speaking, you all just order lots of different dishes and then everyone shares, which is nice. The first time I went out with my wife's family, my father-in-law insisted on paying, which is pretty normal I suppose. What is still a bit strange for me, though, is when you go out with people of your own age and all the men always offer to pay for everything. There's sometimes almost a fight to get hold of the bill first! Generally speaking, back home we just split the bill between everyone.

One final thing I find a bit annoying here is how surprised everyone is that I can use chopsticks. I mean, just because you're foreign, it doesn't mean you can't learn how to use chopsticks!

72

4 She said she was _____ about eating new food before going to Scotland. (not brave)
5 Ya-Wen described blue cheese as _____ cow fat. (rotten)
6 She said she sometimes ordered things that didn't _____ very nice. (end up being)
7 Alan is now happy either pouring olive oil or _____ butter on his bread. (putting)
8 He says people in Britain eat a lot of _____ meals instead of cooking fresh food. (pre-cooked)

5 Work in groups. Discuss the questions.
- Have you ever experienced any of the foods or eating habits mentioned in the texts?
- Does your country share any of the foods or eating habits mentioned in the texts?
- What do you think was the strangest thing mentioned?
- What food and eating habits in your country do you think foreigners might find strange?

ISABELLA (Spanish)

I've been studying in Glasgow for two years now, and it's a great city. When I first moved here, I spent six months living with a host family and they provided me with my first experience of the food. British food has got a bad reputation, but they served great stuff. They introduced me to some really interesting things like the Scottish national dish, haggis. It's a bit like a Spanish blood sausage called *morcilla*, but bigger.

There were a couple of things I just couldn't get used to, though. The first thing was that they always ate everything with bread and butter. It really made me miss olive oil! The other thing was that they used to have dinner at six o'clock every evening. I was starving by bedtime and it didn't give me time to do anything beforehand!

Another cultural difference is that lots of people here go for a drink after work. They tend not to eat while they're drinking, and only get something to eat when the pub finally closes: usually fish and chips, pizzas, that kind of thing. I've even seen deep-fried bars of chocolate! With food like that, it's no wonder there are so many foreign restaurants here!

Having said that, I think I was actually quite unadventurous before coming here, but the Scottish have introduced me to food from other countries – Indian, Thai, Mexican – all of which I love now.

GRAMMAR

Generalisations and *tend to*

We can show that something is generally true by using the structure *tend to* (+ infinitive without *to*), an adverbial phrase like *generally speaking*, or an adverb like *usually* or *hardly*.

6 Look at these sentences from the texts. Answer the questions below.
a *The portions here **tend to be** enormous.*
b *They **tend not to eat** while they're drinking.*
c *People **usually** order things individually for themselves.*
d ***Generally speaking**, back home we just split the bill.*

1 How do you make the negative of *tend to*?
2 Where does an adverbial phrase like *on the whole* or *in general* go in the sentence?
3 Where does an adverb like *normally* go in positive sentences?

G Check your ideas on page 95 and do Exercise 1.

7 Rewrite the sentences using the words in brackets.
1 As a rule, I eat ready meals, because I can't be bothered to cook. (tend)
2 We don't normally keep food which is left over after dinner. (tend)
3 People here tend to eat food with their hands. (general)
4 On the whole, I skip breakfast during the week unless I wake up particularly early. (normally)
5 Generally speaking, our family doesn't eat out unless it's a special occasion. (hardly ever)
6 People don't usually leave tips here unless it was an exceptionally good meal. (rule)
7 I hardly ever have a dessert when I go out for dinner. (tend)
8 Most of the time people here avoid making any noises while they're eating. It's seen as bad manners. (normally)
9 I don't usually have time to have a big lunch, so I normally just have a sandwich. (whole, tend)

8 Work in pairs. Discuss which of the sentences in Exercise 7 are true / not true for you and your country.

I tend not to eat ready meals unless I'm really busy. I normally buy fresh food and cook most evenings.

9 Write five sentences about the culture of your country using *tend* (*not*) *to*. The sentences could be about food, eating, shopping, work, education or character. Then work in groups and compare your ideas. What ideas do you agree with? What ideas are you surprised by?

In the villages, people tend to eat with their right hands, rather than with forks or spoons.

If they have money, most people tend to do most of their shopping in big malls.

Unit 8 Eating 73

WHAT A PLACE!

SPEAKING

1 Work in groups. Discuss the questions.
   - How often do you and your family eat out? Where do you usually go? Why?
   - What's the best / worst restaurant you've ever eaten in? What was so good / bad about it?
   - Are there any restaurants you've never been to but would like to try? Why?

VOCABULARY Restaurants

2 Work in pairs. Read the sentences below and discuss whether you would like to visit each of the restaurants described. Explain your ideas.
   1 It's always **packed**.
   2 It's always **deserted**.
   3 It **looks out over** the sea.
   4 It's got very **trendy décor**.
   5 The **portions** are very **generous**.
   6 The food is beautifully **presented**.
   7 The food's very **rich**.
   8 It's all **organic**.
   9 It's **home-style cooking**.
   10 It only does **seafood**.
   11 It's very fancy, very **posh**.
   12 The **service** is outstanding.

3 Work with a new partner. Think of places you know that fit the descriptions in Exercise 2. Say as much as you can about them to your partner.

LISTENING

4 ▶38 Listen to four conversations about restaurants. Match each conversation (1–4) to one of the topics below. There is one topic you do not need.
   a the restaurant's poor service
   b a crime that's maybe happened
   c sending food back to the kitchen
   d noticing a health issue
   e the quality of the dishes they're eating

5 ▶38 Work in pairs. Choose the correct option. Then listen again and check your answers.
   1 a I was wondering if it might be a *screen* / *front* for something.
     b I don't think I've ever seen *a single* / *an only* person eating there.
   2 a The sauce is quite rich so it really *overcooks* / *overpowers* the taste of everything else.
     b I think I'll *stick* / *stay* with my one.
   3 a It's been in the papers quite *a bit* / *little*.
     b We arrived and sat down and *demanded* / *asked for* the menu.
   4 a The restaurant doesn't *deserve* / *merit* the money.
     b The portions weren't very *great* / *generous*.

GRAMMAR

Second conditionals

We use second conditionals to speculate about situations and possible results. They usually have two parts: an *if*-clause referring to the situation and a second clause showing results or consequences.

6 Look at these sentences from the conversations. Complete the rules below.

a It **wouldn't surprise** me if it **was**.
b I guess it **might be** better if it **didn't have** so much sauce on it.
c You **wouldn't go** there if you **were paying** yourself.
d What **would happen** if they **called** the police?

1 The *if*-clause uses _____ or past continuous.
2 The *if*-clause refers to a situation in the _____ or future which is impossible to change or is not going to take place.
3 The other clause explains the imagined results or consequences. You use _____ + infinitive (without *to*) for a more likely result or _____ + infinitive (without *to*) for a less likely result.

G Check your ideas on page 96 and do Exercise 1.

7 Complete the exchanges with the correct form of the verbs.

1 A: How's the soup?
  B: It's a bit bland, to be honest. It _____ (be) better if it _____ (have) some spices in it.
2 A: Would you like any more?
  B: No. Honestly! I couldn't eat another thing. I _____ (explode) if I _____ (eat) any more!
3 A: They told us we'd have a table in five minutes, but we had to wait for an hour.
  B: That's awful! I hate it when that kind of thing happens. If they just _____ (tell) the truth at times like that, everyone _____ (be) far happier.
4 A: They should do something about the décor. It looks so cold and bare in there.
  B: I know. It _____ (look) a lot more inviting if they _____ (paint) it a warmer colour and _____ (change) the lighting.
5 A: I tasted this crunchy thing in my pasta and spat it out – and then saw it was a fingernail!
  B: Seriously? Oh, that's disgusting! I _____ (die) if that _____ (happen) to me.
6 A: Do you like it? Is it OK?
  B: Yeah. It's delicious! If I _____ (cook) as well as you, I _____ (open) my own restaurant!

PRONUNCIATION

8 ▶39 Listen and write down the six sentences you hear. Look at Track 39 on page 113 and check your answers.

9 ▶39 Listen again and notice the contraction of *would*. Then practise saying the sentences as quickly as you can.

10 Complete the sentences so they are true for you.
1 If I had to wait half an hour to pay the bill, I'd …
2 If I spilt cola all over someone's clothes, I'd …
3 If a waiter was being very rude to me, I'd …
4 If I forgot my wallet and couldn't pay for my meal, I'd …
5 If I was undercharged, I'd …

11 Work in pairs. Ask each other what you would do in each of the situations in Exercise 10. Then ask and answer four more questions starting with *What would you do if* …?

G For further practice, see Exercise 2 on page 96.

SPEAKING

12 Below are eight sentences connected to food and drink. Decide if you agree or disagree with each one – and why. Think about what the results of each could be.

If they banned the sale of chocolate, …
… shops would lose a lot of money
… it might damage the economy
… people might lose their jobs, etc.

1 If they want to improve public health, they should ban the sale of chocolate and ice cream.
2 School students should be given two free pieces of fruit a day at school.
3 The legal age for drinking should be raised to 21.
4 All the extra food produced in rich countries should be donated to developing countries.
5 Children should discuss issues connected to nutrition more in school.
6 Fast food restaurants should be taxed more – and the money should go towards health care.
7 The government should stop telling me what to eat and how to live. It's not their job!
8 People who get ill because they eat or drink too much should pay more for health care.

13 Work in groups. Compare your opinions about the sentences in Exercise 12. Use second conditionals and some of the language below.

- It's not a bad idea.
- I agree with this up to a point.
- That's completely mad! / That's a stupid idea!
- Can you imagine what would happen if they did that?
- If they did that, they'd create all kinds of problems. For example, …
- It'd solve a few problems. For example, …

Unit 8   Eating   75

VIDEO 4

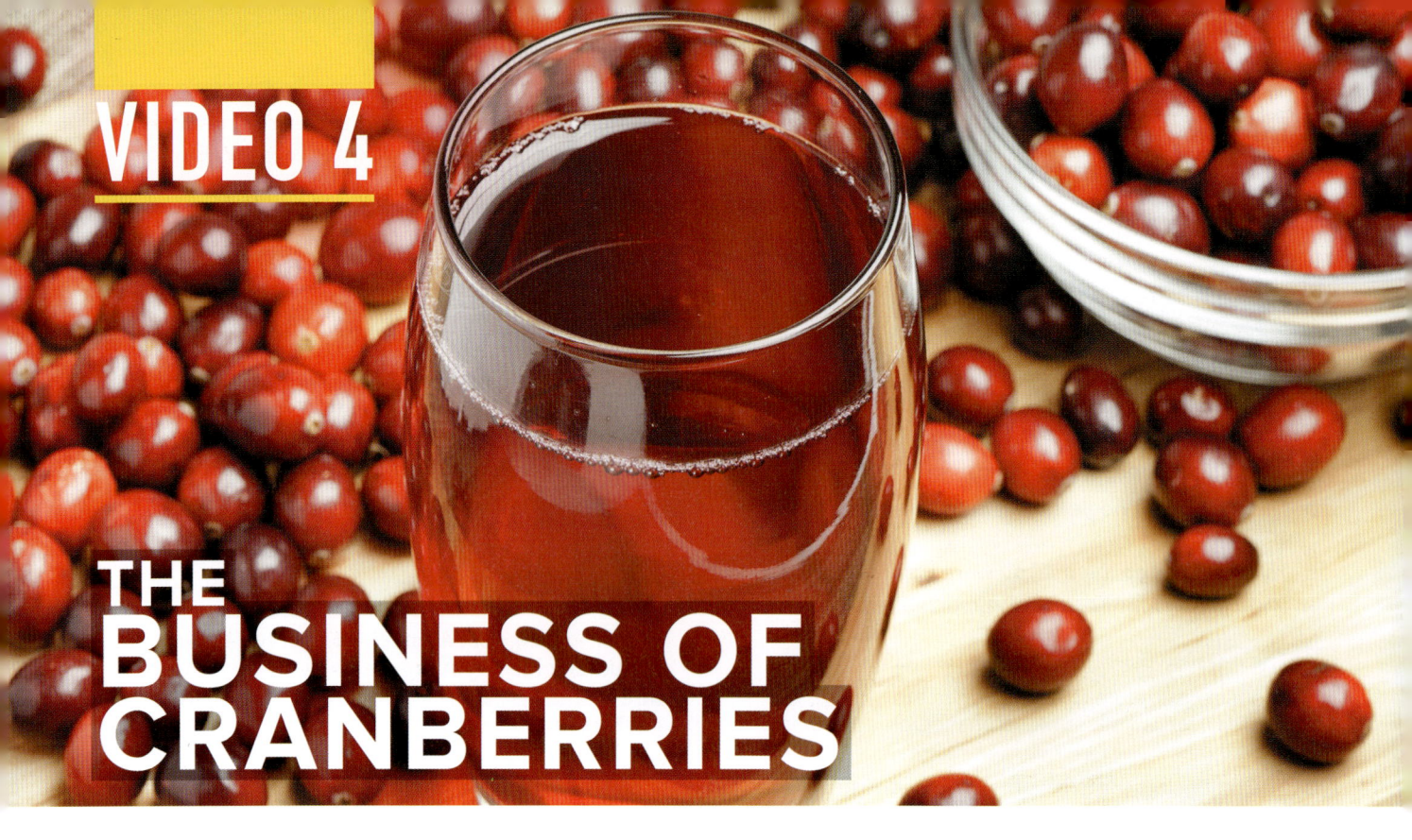

THE BUSINESS OF CRANBERRIES

1 **Work in groups. Look at the photo and discuss the questions.**
   - Do you eat much fruit or drink much fruit juice? Why? / Why not?
   - What fruits are grown in your country? In what area?
   - Have you ever eaten cranberries? Did you like them?
   - What do you know about where they grow and what the tree / plant is like?
   - How do you think they are harvested?

2 **▶ 15 Watch the first part of the video (0.00–2.24). Are the sentences true (T) or false (F)?**
   1 Mary's job starts at dawn.
   2 Mary always wanted to have both a career and a family.
   3 The cranberry vines live on average for seventeen years.
   4 Mary is the boss of the cranberry business.
   5 Cranmoor is the biggest producer of inland cranberries in the world.
   6 To grow well, cranberries like water, acid conditions and sand.
   7 Mary inherited the cranberry farm.

3 **Work in pairs. Discuss the questions.**
   - In what ways is Mary lucky?
   - Do you know anyone who is similar to Mary in any way? How?
   - Would you like to be her? Why? / Why not?

4 **▶ 15 Read the short summary of how they harvest the cranberries. Then watch the second part of the video and complete the summary with one or two words in each space (2.25–4.04).**

When the berries ripen in early fall, the growers ^{1}_____ the marsh beds. They use machines called ^{2}_____ to remove the berries, which then float to the surface and are collected together.

They have to keep an eye on ^{3}_____ because a hard frost can destroy the crop.

When the berries are in danger of ^{4}_____ , the growers turn on an irrigation system to keep the temperature above ^{5}_____ and to produce a bumper crop.

^{6}_____ , dykes and ditches store water to provide an adequate supply at a ^{7}_____ .

Mary thinks the cranberry harvest is not just good for her business but also good for ^{8}_____ . She sees herself as a mother to both her children and the environment in which she lives.

5 **Work in groups. Discuss the questions.**
   - In which areas of your country is there most farming? What are the main crops?
   - Have there been any problems for crops in recent years because of the weather? What happened?
   - Do you think farming benefits or damages wildlife in your country? In what ways?

UNDERSTANDING FAST SPEECH

6 **▶ 16 Read and listen to this extract from the video said at natural pace and then slowed down. To help you, groups of words are marked with / and pauses are marked //. Stressed sounds are in CAPITALS.**

when PEOple would ASK me / what I WANted to BE / when I grew UP / I KNEW / all aLONG / there were TWO things I WANted to DO // um / be a MOM // and WORK outSIDE.

7 **Now you have a go! Practise saying the extract at natural pace.**

REVIEW 4

GRAMMAR

1 Complete the text with one word in each space. Contractions count as one word.

Generally ¹_____ , when I was growing up we had a traditional Sunday lunch. As a ²_____ , my mum cooked some roast meat like chicken or beef served ³_____ some boiled vegetables and a sauce which we call *gravy*. I loved it, but now I live on my own I ⁴_____ ever have a Sunday lunch ⁵_____ I visit my parents. Basically, cooking a roast dinner takes a long time and I'm usually too tired on Sunday as I ⁶_____ to go out till late on Saturday. Maybe if I ⁷_____ cooking for more than one person I ⁸_____ make an effort, but it's not worth it just for me. Maybe ⁹_____ I ever get married and ¹⁰_____ my own family, ¹¹_____ make them a proper Sunday lunch, but I bet it ¹²_____ taste as good as my mum's.

2 Choose **all** the correct options.

1 If you are ill, *take / you should take / you would take* a day off.
2 If they *improved / improve / have improved* the décor, maybe more people would come in.
3 Hopefully, I'll get a job after *I graduate / I'll graduate / I have graduated*.
4 If I don't find anything soon, *I might look / I'll look / I look* for a job abroad somewhere.
5 I *almost never / tend not / don't tend to* eat out. It's just too expensive.
6 I'll let you know *as soon as / when / if* I hear anything.
7 I'll call you *when / once / if* I'm ready.
8 What if he *finds out / found out / will find out*?

3 Complete the second sentence so that it has a similar meaning to the first sentence using the word given. Do not change the word given. You must use between three and five words, including the word given.

1 My main meal of the day tends to be lunch.
   _____ my main meal in the middle of the day. **WHOLE**
2 First, I'm going to speak to this gentleman. Then I'll deal with your problem.
   I'll deal with your problem _____ to this gentleman. **ONCE**
3 He'll never pass his final exams because he hardly ever goes to class.
   If he _____ classes, he might actually pass his final exams. **SKIP**
4 The only reason you are allowed to miss a deadline is serious illness.
   We _____ if you are seriously ill. **EXTEND**
5 My plan is to retire at the age of 60.
   I'm _____ I'm 60. **WORK**
6 I'm lucky that my parents can afford to pay for my university fees.
   I _____ university now if my parents didn't have the money to pay the fees. **BE**

4 🔊 40 Listen and write the six sentences you hear.

5 Write a sentence before and after the sentences from Exercise 4 to create short dialogues.

VOCABULARY

6 Match the verbs (1–8) with the noun (a–h) they both collocate with.

1 make / slow my   a an excuse
2 pay / give plenty of   b progress
3 make / accept   c an assignment
4 ask for / split   d the bill
5 have / hand in   e my motivation to study
6 lose / increase   f the fish
7 give / receive good   g attention to someone
8 marinate / steam   h feedback

7 Decide if these words are connected to food / restaurants or teachers / courses.

bland	fee	mash	patient
deserted	grate	module	raw
discipline	lecture	organic	supportive

8 Complete the sentences. Use the word in brackets to form a word that fits in the space.

1 The university has lowered its _____ requirements to attract more students. (enter)
2 I have to say, the course didn't really meet my _____ . (expect)
3 It's more important to be _____ and have passion than have high _____ . (enthuse, qualify)
4 The school has faced a lot of _____ over its pupils' poor exam _____ . (criticise, perform).
5 It needs to adopt an _____ approach to improve students' grades. (alter)
6 The headteacher went on a course to improve his _____ , but he's still not very good! (leader)
7 The initial results of the changes are quite _____ and there are many signs of _____ . (encourage, improve)
8 They said her coursework was _____ – some of the best they'd had. (stand out)

9 Complete the extract from an email with one word in each space. The first letters are given.

Did I tell you Tim's gone back to college to ¹tr_____ as a chef? As you know, he ²str_____ at school, but he's doing really well on this course. Obviously, the course is very ³pr_____ so most of the lessons are ⁴wor_____ to learn the skills they need such as ⁵sl_____ vegetables quickly without chopping your fingers off! But he's even enjoying the more ⁶ac_____ subjects like maths and biology. I guess it's because they make them ⁷re_____ to what he wants to do, which is to have a good business and not poison anyone! Anyway, the college has a restaurant and we went last week. It doesn't look very ⁸fa_____ – I don't think they've changed the décor for years – but the food was amazing. I had this lamb which had been ⁹ro_____ really slowly, so it was so juicy and ¹⁰te_____ . And it came with a lovely ¹¹ri_____ sauce – fantastic. The meal was actually part of Tim's ¹²as_____ and of course he passed! I was so proud of him.

Review 4   77

1 WRITING Keeping in touch

SPEAKING

1 Work in pairs. Discuss the questions.
- Are you good at keeping in touch with people? Why? / Why not?
- What's good and bad about these ways of keeping in touch?
  - email
  - phone
  - Facebook (or similar)
  - WhatsApp (or similar)
- Think of someone you know who you haven't been in touch with for a while. Why haven't you been in touch? What was their situation last time you were in touch? Do you know if it has changed at all? In what way?

WRITING

2 Read an email from an Italian student, Chiara, to a Chinese friend she met while studying in the UK. Put the parts (a–g) into the correct order. Then work in pairs and explain your order.

3 Use words from the email to complete the phases that we often use in emails when catching up with news.
1 How are you? Sorry I haven't _____ recently, but I've _____ very busy.
2 When I _____ wrote I told you …
3 _____ what? We're getting married!
4 _____ , what about you? What _____ you doing at the _____ ?
5 I often think _____ you and the great _____ we had.
6 Write to me _____ and tell me your _____ .

4 Work in groups. Discuss the questions.
- Do you think Chiara and Hugo have decided to get married too quickly? Why? / Why not?
- Would you like to study abroad? Why? / Why not?
- Do you have any friends from other countries? How did you meet?
- Apart from emails, what ways can you think of to practise writing in English? What's the best way?

To   Lian@hotmail.ml
From   Chiara@hotmail.ml

Dear Lian,

a **Apart from** getting married, looking for a flat and working six nights a week, I'm also going to the gym a lot. I want to get fit and lose some weight so I look good in my wedding dress. And that's another thing I need to do – get my wedding dress! I'm completely exhausted, but I'm **also** really happy!

b Lots of love

c When I last wrote, I told you I'd met a guy called Hugo. Well, guess what? We're getting married! He proposed when we were having a meal to celebrate our first six months together. I know it seems quick, but he's a really wonderful guy. It now looks as if I'm going to stay in Scotland for a long time!

d Anyway, what about you? What are you doing at the moment? When you wrote last, you said you were feeling a bit tired and you were thinking of taking a holiday and going to see Eri in Japan. Did you go? How was it? How is Eri? I often think of you and her and the great times we had at school here. It would be great if you could come and visit.

e Write to me soon and tell me your news.

f How are you? Sorry I haven't written recently, but I've been very busy. So many things are happening in my life at the moment it's difficult to find time for anything else!

g **As well as** getting married, we're looking for a new place to live. We want to find a house – somewhere nice where we can start a family. It's very expensive here, so it's good that I **also** started a new job two months ago. I'm working in an Italian restaurant. The basic wages aren't great, but I usually get a lot of tips, so the money could be worse. The owner is Scottish. His grandparents were Italian, but he doesn't speak Italian very well, so it's good for my English **too**. And, of course, I speak English with Hugo and his family. Before I met his parents, I was very nervous, but they're very kind and friendly.

Chiara

KEY WORDS FOR WRITING

as well as, apart from, too and also

We use *as well as* and *apart from* to join ideas and different parts of sentences. Notice how these phrases can start a sentence and that they are followed by an *-ing* form without a subject pronoun. At the end of the clause starting with *as well as / apart from*, add a comma.

As well as getting married, we're looking for a new place to live.

Apart from getting married, looking for a flat and working six nights a week, I'm also going to the gym a lot.

Too and *also* add ideas, but you need another word such as *and*, *but* or *so* to join the two parts of a sentence. *Too* goes at the end of the sentence / clause. *Also* usually goes in the middle.

I am exhausted, **but** I'm **also** really happy.

He doesn't speak Italian very well, **so** it's good for my English **too**.

It's very expensive here, **so** it's good that I **also** started a new job two months ago.

5 Join the pairs of sentences using the words in brackets and making any other necessary changes.
1 I started a new job last week. I'm moving house. (also)
2 I'm studying a lot. I'm training hard for a marathon. (as well as)
3 My brother is living with me at the moment. I'm busy looking after him. (too)
4 I helped to organise my mum's 50th birthday party. I've been busy at work. (apart from)
5 I went to Germany on holiday. I went to Sweden for a conference recently. (as well as)
6 Quite a lot of bad things have happened. I have some good news. (too)

6 Write three sentences about your recent life using *too / also* or *as well as / apart from*. Then read your sentences to a partner.

GRAMMAR

Reporting what people said

When we write to catch up with news, we often refer to the situation the last time we wrote to / spoke to / saw the person we're writing to. Notice how we use the past perfect simple or the past continuous to show if the action happened before we spoke, or around the same time.

The other week when I saw you, I remember you said your mum **was** *ill.* (= ill at the time we met)

When I last wrote, I told you I **had met** *a guy called Hugo.* (= We met before I wrote.)

When you wrote last, you said you **were feeling** *a bit tired and you* **were thinking** *of taking a holiday and going to see Eri in Japan* (= You were thinking around the same time as you wrote.)

7 Complete the sentences with the correct auxiliary forms. To do this, you will need to decide if the action took place before or around the same time that you wrote / spoke. Note that you may need to use negative forms.
1 The last time you wrote, I think you told me you _____ started a new job.
2 The last time I wrote to you, I think I _____ still pregnant.
3 The last time we spoke, you said you _____ feeling a bit down.
4 The last time I saw you, you _____ doing your exams.
5 The last time I saw you, I _____ have a job.
6 The last time you wrote, you said you _____ planning to move.
7 The last time we spoke, I still _____ graduated.
8 The last time I wrote, I _____ going out with Karen.

8 Match sentences 1–8 from Exercise 7 with the follow-up comments / questions a–h.
a How are you now? I hope you're better.
b How's it going? Are you finding it easier?
c Did you find anywhere nice? What's your new address?
d How did you do? Did you pass them all?
e Well, Sara is two now and I'm actually expecting my second!
f Well, guess what? I'm now the assistant manager of a local store.
g Well, unfortunately we've split up.
h Well, I finished last July and now I'm doing a Master's.

9 Complete the sentences with your own ideas. Then add a follow-up question or comment.
1 The last time you wrote, you said …
2 The last time I saw you, I think I …
3 The last time I spoke to her, …

PRACTICE

10 You are going to write an email to someone who you haven't been in touch with for a while. You want to catch up with their news. Before you write, think about the following.
- why you haven't been in touch
- the situation you were both in when you last spoke and / or what you talked about
- your situation now; things you're doing; events that have happened to you recently
- questions you want to ask your friend

11 Write your email. Use the model email to help you and use as much language from this lesson as you can.

Writing 79

2 WRITING Short emails

SPEAKING

1 Work in pairs. Discuss the questions.
- How often do you check your email?
- How many emails a day do you think you send?
- Who do you write to most often?
- Do you ever send emails in English? Who to? Why?

WRITING

Explaining why you are writing

We generally begin emails with a line explaining why we are writing. To people we already know, we often begin with sentence starters like this:

Just a	quick	one	to let you know
	short	note	to remind
		email	to ask
			to tell
			to say I'm sorry
			to say thank you
			to say congratulations

All of these sentence starters can be used with friends or with colleagues. However, in more formal contexts, it may be best to avoid the word *one* and use *note* or *email* instead.

2 Complete the pairs of sentence endings 1–7 with sentence starters from the box.

1. ... you that next Monday is a public holiday.
   ... you to bring that book you said you'd lend me.
2. ... I missed you while you were in Paris.
   ... to hear you've been ill.
3. ... for all your hard work organising the conference.
   ... for a lovely weekend.
4. ... I arrived safely in Hong Kong.
   ... I'll be a bit late to the meeting tomorrow.
5. ... if you could do me a big favour.
   ... if you could send me the photos you took at the party.
6. ... you I can't make the meeting tomorrow.
   ... you how much we enjoyed the barbecue last night.
7. ... on your exam results.
   ... to you both. The baby's beautiful.

3 Work in pairs. Write one more possible ending for each of the seven sentence starters in the box above.

4 Complete the three short emails with the correct whole sentence from Exercise 2.

1

Dear Thorsten,

_____ I'm planning to come to Germany next month on business and need to contact Matthias Einhoff before I arrive. I want to arrange a meeting with him to discuss a new project. The problem is, though, I've lost his contact details. Do you know anyone who might have them? I'd be really grateful if you could try to find out.

Anyway, I hope all is well – and hope to hear from you soon.

Many thanks,

Oliver

2

Hi Lars

_____ I think you arrived the day after I had to go to Vienna for a friend's wedding. I was there for three days and had a great time, and then came back on the 27th and tried to call you, but I got a message saying the number wasn't available. Have you changed your mobile or lost it or something?

Anyway, I hope you had fun here and please let me know in advance next time you're planning to come here again. I would love to see you again. It's been a long time!

All the best,

Maria

3

Hi Tatsu,

_____ I can't believe you got an A! You must be really pleased. Still, after all your hard work, you deserve it! I hope you're going to go out and celebrate. I've got my exams next month and am really worried about them. I just hope I do as well as you did.

Anyway, write to me when you have a free minute and tell me all your news.

Cheers for now,

Davorka

SPEAKING

5 Work in pairs. Discuss the questions.
- Have you ever lost anyone's contact details? How did you lose them? Did you manage to get them back again?
- Have you been to a wedding in the last few years? When? Whose was it? What was it like?
- Have you congratulated anyone recently? Why?
- Have you got any exams in the near future? Do you know anyone else who has?

GRAMMAR

Leaving out words

When we add information to a sentence using *and / or*, we often leave words out if they have already been used. We assume the missing words are understood by the reader.

I'm planning to come to Germany next month on business and (I) need to contact Matthias Einhoff before I arrive.

6 Decide which words have been left out of these sentences. Then work in pairs. Compare your answers. What kinds of words are generally left out?
1 Have you changed your mobile or lost it or something?
2 I've got my exams next month and am already really worried about them.
3 I hope this is OK with you and won't cause too many problems.
4 I will talk to Rose on Thursday and ask her what I missed, but please do let me know if there's anything urgent I need to do or know about before then.

7 Rewrite each of the groups of sentences below as one sentence. Link your ideas using *and / or*. Leave out any words you think are unnecessary.
1 We left Sydney on Friday night. We arrived in Hong Kong on Saturday morning.
2 I really want to send one of the photos to my mum. I want to burn some of the other photos onto a CD.
3 Don't worry about missing class tomorrow. Don't worry about taking time off if you need to.
4 Don't feel you have to wear a suit to the party tonight. Don't feel you have to bring a present.
5 I'm going to Prague tomorrow. I'm going to Pisa on Friday, so I won't be at the meeting on Thursday. I won't be at work for the rest of this week.
6 I thought the story was great. I thought the acting was really good, but I didn't really like the ending. I didn't really like some of the songs.

VOCABULARY

Ending emails

The way we end emails depends on who we are writing to. Some endings are more common for formal emails, while others are more common for neutral or informal ones.

8 Look at these nine different ways of ending emails. Work in pairs. Discuss which endings you could use:
1 in more formal situations (e.g. applying for a job, writing to someone you don't know at all).
2 in more neutral situations (e.g. colleagues at work, people you already know).
3 in more informal situations (e.g. close friends and family).

Kind regards	Love	Lots of love
Yours faithfully	All the best	Cheers for now
Many thanks	Yours sincerely	Yours

9 Work in pairs. Think of the letters and emails that you send. Which of the endings in Exercise 8 could you use if you wrote them in English? Say as much as you can about who your emails are to, and which endings you would use.

PRACTICE

10 Write four short emails. Begin each one with a sentence starter from the Writing box. Try to write two more informal emails, and two more formal ones. Use as much of the language from this lesson as you can.

Writing 81

3 WRITING Stories

SPEAKING

1. You are going to read a short story written for an exam. It starts with the line: *It was dangerous, but I knew I had to do it.* First, work in pairs and do the following.
   - Based on this first line, think of four possible things that the writer was about to do.
   - How do you think each of these four stories might then develop?

WRITING A story

2. The four sentences below are from the story. Check you understand the words in bold. Then work in pairs. Discuss the order you expect to read the sentences in. Explain your ideas.
   a I could feel the wind **rushing** past me as I fell.
   b I **floated** slowly down.
   c I moved my feet closer to the **edge** and looked down!
   d Eventually, I pulled the **cord**.

3. Now read the story and complete it with the correct form (past simple, past continuous or past perfect simple) of the verbs. Then work in pairs and compare your ideas.

SPEAKING

4. Work in pairs. Discuss the questions.
   - Do you know anyone who has done a parachute jump?
   - Would you like to do one? Why? / Why not?
   - Would you like to do any of these other dangerous things? Are there any you have done already?
     - go whitewater rafting
     - go mountaineering
     - do a bungee jump
     - go hang-gliding
     - hitchhike round the world
     - explore caves

It was dangerous, but I knew I had to do it. If there is one thing I love, it's a challenge. I moved my feet closer to the edge and looked down. I was just about to jump when it suddenly hit me. I was really going to do it! Nobody had believed me when I ¹_____ (say) I would do it, but there I was.

I moved my feet closer to the edge and looked down. It was a very long way to the ground! Everyone else ²_____ (seem) so relaxed, but my heart ³_____ (beat) like crazy. Just as I ⁴_____ (think) about maybe changing my mind, the voice behind me ⁵_____ (scream), 'Go! Go! Go!' – so I jumped.

Suddenly, the panic and the fear just disappeared. I ⁶_____ (really / fly)! I could feel the wind rushing past me as I fell. Eventually, I pulled the cord on my parachute and it ⁷_____ (open) – thankfully! I floated slowly down, enjoying the incredible views. I ⁸_____ (land) safely and knew at once that this was something I wanted to do again.

KEY WORDS FOR WRITING

just about to, just as

Was / Were (just) about to + infinitive (without to) is used to talk about something you were planning to do before something else happened. When suddenly often follows just about to.

*I **was just about to jump when suddenly** it hit me!*

Just as is used to emphasise that two verbs happened at exactly the same time. It is more common to use the past continuous after *just as* but the past simple is also possible.

***Just as I was thinking** about maybe changing my mind, the voice behind me screamed, 'Go! Go! Go!'*

***Just as I turned on** the computer, I heard a bang and the lights went out.*

5 Match the two parts of the sentences.
1 I was just about to give up and stop looking
2 She was just about to go back to bed
3 We were just about to kiss
4 Just as the band appeared on the stage,
5 Just as we were all sitting down to eat dinner,
6 Just as I was walking out of the store,

a when she suddenly heard a strange noise downstairs.
b three men ran in, holding guns and pushed past me.
c when suddenly I saw something shiny in the dirt.
d there was a loud knock at the door.
e when my ex-boyfriend suddenly walked in.
f the woman next to me started screaming like crazy!

6 Work in pairs. Think of one more possible ending for each of the sentence beginnings 1–6 in Exercise 5.

7 Rewrite each pair of sentences as one sentence. Link your ideas using the words in brackets. Make any other changes you think are necessary.
1 We were planning to leave. Then they gave us a table. (just about to)
_____
2 I was planning to give up and go home. Then I saw him walking towards me. (just about to)
_____
3 I was planning to go to bed. Then the doorbell rang. (just about to)
_____
4 We were walking towards our car. A police car suddenly drove up and stopped right in front of us. (just as)
_____
5 We were starting to think the holiday was going to be a disaster. At that moment, the sun came out. (just as)
_____

VOCABULARY

Descriptive verbs

We can use descriptive verbs to make stories more exciting.

*The voice behind me **screamed**, 'Go! Go! Go!'*

8 Match the descriptive verbs 1–7 with their definitions a–g.
1 slam   a say very quietly
2 grab   b move very quietly / slowly
3 shout   c look at something for a long time
4 stare   d close; put something down angrily / loudly
5 rush   e say very loudly
6 creep   f run; go in a hurry
7 whisper   g take hold with your hand suddenly

9 Work in pairs. Take turns to act the words from Exercise 8. Can your partner guess what you are doing?

10 Complete the sentences with the correct form of the verbs from Exercise 8.
1 The train was leaving in ten minutes so we _____ to the station.
2 He ran out and _____ the door shut behind him.
3 I _____ at the paper. I couldn't believe what it said.
4 Just as I was leaving, someone _____ my bag and ran off.
5 It was chaos. Everyone was screaming and _____ .
6 I _____ down the stairs, trying not to make a noise.
7 I tried to _____ the answer to my friend but the teacher heard me.

PRACTICE

11 Look at the exam questions below and choose one.
a Write a story that starts with one of the following lines:
  - It was three o'clock in the morning when the phone rang.
  - It was dangerous, but I knew I had to do it.
b Write a story that ends with one of the following lines:
  - … and that was the best day of my life.
  - … and that was the worst day of my life.

12 Plan your story. Then work in pairs and discuss your ideas. Can you think of any ways to make the story more exciting?

13 Write the story. Use between 150 and 180 words.

Writing 83

4 WRITING Making requests

SPEAKING

1 Check you understand the words in bold. Then work in pairs and discuss the questions.
- When was the last time you **did** a friend **a favour**? What was it?
- When was the last time you **asked** a friend **to do you a favour**? What was it? How did you ask? What did they say?
- Do you **owe** anyone **a favour** at the moment?

GRAMMAR

Indirect questions
In writing, we often avoid direct requests and questions. Notice how the word order changes after the indirect question phrase. For example:

Can you send me the files as soon as possible? →

Do you think you could send me the files as soon as possible?

How much is it? →

Could you tell me how much *it is*?

2 Complete the indirect questions by putting the words in brackets in the correct order.
 1 **Could you do me a favour and** _____ (it / now / for / buy / me) and then I'll pay you back later?
 2 **Do you think** _____ (could / ring / give / him / a / you) and speak to him about it?
 3 **Is there any way** _____ (letter / could / this / you / translate) for me?
 4 **I was wondering** _____ (could / if / me / you / send / possibly) some samples of your work?
 5 **Could you tell me** _____ (everything / when / be / will / collect / to / ready)?

3 Write a different ending for each of the five indirect question starters in bold in Exercise 2.

WRITING

4 Read these four emails and complete them with one word in each space.

5 Work in pairs. Discuss these questions for each email.
- Who is writing to whom?
- What phrase(s) are used to say thank you?
- Do you think the requests are reasonable? If not, why not?
- Are there any requests you would not ask or would refuse to do? Why?

1

Dear Sir/Madam,

I have already ¹_____ a reservation under the name of Rosario for the 18th–20th January. Would it be possible to stay an extra night on Saturday 21st January? If not, do you ²_____ you could inform me as ³_____ as possible as I will then need to make other arrangements.

Many thanks.

Yours faithfully,

Sandra Rosario

2

Hi Zarina,

Just a quick one to ¹_____ thank you for the email. I love the photos! Is there any ²_____ you could print them out, though, as my printer isn't very good? I'd ³_____ to frame the photos and put them on my wall.

Michaele

3

Dear Margot,

Long time, no see. How are you? I've been very ¹_____ finishing my final dissertation for my Master's. It's 20,000 words, so I haven't been out much! I've attached it here. As your English is so good, could you do me a big ²_____ and look through it carefully to check it's OK? I'd ³_____ really grateful.

Cheers,

Olaf

4

Dear Mario,

Just a quick email to ¹_____ you know when I'll be arriving in Milan. The flight gets in at 05.10 on Friday morning. Actually, I was ²_____ if you could possibly come and pick me up, if it's not too much trouble? I'd be really grateful as I'll have loads of luggage.

³_____ the best,

Andre

84

VOCABULARY

Synonyms

In the first email, Sandra asks if they can *inform her as soon as possible*. *Inform* is a synonym for *tell*. We can use synonyms to make something sound more formal or more 'chatty', but often there is no difference in formality.

6 Match the verbs in italics 1–8 with their synonyms a–h. Which verbs are more formal?

1 *request* a refund
2 *collect* Maria from the airport
3 the flight *arrives* at five
4 *inform* me when it is ready
5 *enquire* about prices
6 *complete* the form
7 *forward* the email to him
8 *apologise* for the error

a pick up
b send on
c get in
d fill in
e ask for
f say sorry
g ask
h tell

7 Work in pairs. Tell each other about the last time you:
 • requested something by email.
 • informed someone of something by email.
 • enquired about something by email.
 • completed a form.
 • sent on an email, message or link.
 • apologised for something.

KEYWORDS FOR WRITING

as

We saw in Writing 3 that *as / just as* is sometimes used to mean *while*. *As* is also very commonly used to mean *because*.

As your English is so good, could you do me a big favour and look through it carefully to check it's OK?

I'd be really grateful **as** I'll have loads of luggage.

As is also used in certain common expressions.

Do you think you could inform me **as soon as possible**?

8 Use the ideas below to write five requests and add reasons using *as*. Use one of the expressions from Exercise 5 to say thanks.

look after the kids?

Is there any way you could look after the kids on Friday as we have tickets for the theatre? We'd be really grateful.

1 send me another copy of the invoice?
2 give me a lift?
3 stay at your place for a few days?
4 extend the deadline for my essay?
5 complete the work by Thursday?

9 Complete the sentences below with these expressions.

a as far as I know
b as far as the hotel is concerned
c as soon as you hear
d as soon as you arrive
e as quickly as you can
f as soon as possible

1 Do you think you could email me _____ any news as I'm a bit worried about him?
2 When you arrive, you need to go _____ to Terminal B as there isn't much time for the transfer between flights.
3 Give me a call _____ at the station and I'll come and pick you up. Just wait outside the main entrance.
4 _____ , it's all booked and confirmed. Is there any way you could sort out the car hire, though, as I don't have a driving licence?
5 Could you let me know _____ whether you can come or not as we need to make the booking?
6 _____ , the shuttle bus runs all night, but perhaps you should ring the tourist information office to check.

PRACTICE

10 Work in pairs. First, working on your own, write two short emails making requests. One should be to a hotel or company and the other should be to your partner. Use as much language from this lesson as you can.

11 Swap your emails with your partner. Write a reply to each one.

GRAMMAR REFERENCE

1 FIRST CLASS

AUXILIARY VERBS

do

We use forms of the verb *do* with the infinitive (without *to*).
Do you **like** Indian food? (present simple)
We **don't live** very near each other. (present simple)
Does your brother **live** near you? (present simple)
He **doesn't** really **like** this kind of music. (present simple)
Did you **have** a good time last night? (past simple)
I **didn't go** anywhere last night. (past simple)

have

We use forms of the verb *have* with the past participle form of the verb.
Have you ever **eaten** snake? (present perfect simple)
Has your brother **been** to Lisbon before? (present perfect simple)
I **haven't been** there. (present perfect simple)

be

We use forms of the verb *be* with the *-ing* form of the verb.
What **are** you **studying**? (present continuous)
She **isn't feeling** very well. (present continuous)
Where **were** you **living** at the time? (past continuous)
What **was** she **doing** in Kazakhstan? (past continuous)

Notice how we combine *have* and *been* to form the present perfect continuous.
How long **have** you **been studying** English?
He **hasn't been working** there very long.

We also use the verb *be* with the past participle to make passive forms of the verb.
What language **is** that **written** in? (present simple)
When **was** this film **made**? (past simple)

Exercise 1

Choose the correct option.

1 I heard you were ill yesterday. *Is / Are / Does* you feeling better now?
2 *Do / Does* you and your sister get on OK?
3 Where *did you / were you* born?
4 *Did / Have / Were* you visited many foreign countries?
5 *Have / Has / Is* your parents met your girlfriend yet?
6 Where *were / did / does* your parents first meet?
7 How long *you been / have you been* waiting?
8 How long *is / have / has / does* he been married?

Exercise 2

Make negative sentences by adding the correct auxiliary + *not* / *-n't*.

1 She _____ working today, I'm afraid. I think she's sick.
2 Can we go somewhere else? I _____ really like this place very much.
3 I don't see my sister very often. She _____ live very near me.
4 I _____ working at the moment. I need to find a job!
5 When I told them, they _____ believe me. They said I was lying!

6 We _____ going away anywhere during the holidays. We're just staying at home.
7 He _____ studied for his exams at all! He's going to fail!
8 She went home because she _____ feeling very well.
9 I feel bad because I _____ done the homework for today.
10 He speaks really well given that he _____ been studying for that long.

In the examples and exercises above, you have met different forms. You will meet all these forms again in the book.

Past simple and past continuous	Unit 1
Present simple and continuous	Unit 2
Present perfect simple and past simple	Unit 3
Present perfect continuous and past simple	Unit 4
Present perfect simple and continuous	Unit 9
Passives	Unit 11

NARRATIVE TENSES

Past simple

Add *-ed* to the infinitive (without *to*). Some past forms are irregular, such as *spoke*, *fell* and *met*. To make a negative, use *didn't* + infinitive (without *to*). The past simple is the most common tense used when telling stories. It shows the events followed each other in order.
I **heard** a noise and **turned** round to look. I **didn't see** the hole in front of me and so I **tripped** and **fell**. I **hurt** my knee quite badly.

Past continuous

Use *was / were* + *-ing* form.
I / She / He **was(n't) waiting** for a long time.
It **was(n't) raining** outside.
You / We / They **were(n't) working**.

We often use the past continuous at the beginning of the story to give background information – the events taking place around the time of the story.
Something similar happened to me when I **was living** in Dubai. One day, I was at work …
Anyway, last year I **was filming** in Sumatra and at dinner one day …

The past continuous shows an action was unfinished or stopped by another action.
I **was walking** down the street when I heard a noise behind me. I turned round to look and tripped and fell. (= I fell before I got to the end of the street.)

Past perfect simple

Use *had* + past participle.
I / She / We / They etc. **had(n't) seen** the film before.
  had(n't) spoken to him.

The past perfect shows the 'past in the past' – an action that happened before something else we already talked about. It often goes with words like *previously*, *already* or *before*.
I suddenly remembered I **hadn't turned off** the cooker, so I went back home, but by the time I got there, the kitchen **had already caught** fire.
I knew quite a lot of people in the music industry because I'd **previously been** in a band.

86

Exercise 1

Match six sentence starters from 1–12 with the sentence endings a–f. There are six sentence starters you don't need.

1. I was really surprised he failed the exam because
2. I asked them to turn the music down because
3. He didn't post the letter because
4. He didn't post the letter, even though
5. We were running out of petrol, so
6. We ran out of petrol, so
7. When she told us she was thinking of becoming a model,
8. I think she got upset because
9. By the time we got there the show had already started, so
10. When we got there the show was just starting, so
11. I met my girlfriend while
12. I met my girlfriend and then

a. we stopped at a garage.
b. he'd studied a lot.
c. we went to a friend's for dinner.
d. we didn't really miss much.
e. I'd reminded him at least three times.
f. we were laughing at her.

Exercise 2

Complete the story with the correct form of the verbs.

I remember a mistake I made when I ¹_____ (teach) English in Argentina. I ²_____ (learn) a bit of Spanish before in the UK, but I wasn't very accurate or fluent. Anyway, I was in class one day trying to get the students to talk, but they ³_____ (not / say) anything, so I said in Spanish, 'Don't get embarrassed! We all make mistakes. Just try.' The students ⁴_____ (look) surprised and said 'Embarazada?' 'Yes,' I said, 'I know how you feel because I'm a Spanish student and I'm embarrassed too sometimes.' I later found out I ⁵_____ (not / use) the right word – *embarazada* actually means pregnant! After that being 'embarrassed' ⁶_____ (become) a joke in class and I never ⁷_____ (make) that mistake again! Funnily enough, though, the students actually ⁸_____ (start) talking a bit more English in class as a result.

2 FEELINGS

LINKING VERBS

The most common linking verbs are *be, look, seem, feel, sound, taste* and *smell*. After these linking verbs, we use one pattern when they are followed by an adjective and different patterns when they are followed by a clause or a noun.

Linking verb + adjective

The verbs can be followed by an adjective without adding any other words (apart from adding modifiers like *very, a bit,* etc. to the adjective).

*I **feel fine**.*   *This cake **tastes strange**.*
*He **looked a bit upset**.*

Linking verb + clause

When these verbs are followed by a clause, the verbs can be followed by *as if* or *like*.
*You **look as if** you're in a very good mood. How come?*
*I **feel** guilty. I **feel as if** it's my fault.*
*You **sound like** you're better.*

DID YOU KNOW?
Like and *as if* mean the same thing in this context. However, some people believe that using *like* with clauses is wrong or too informal. In exams and when writing, it may be better to use *as if*.

Linking verb + noun

When these verbs are followed by a noun, add *like*. It means *the same as,* or *similar to*.
*She **looks like** a model!*   *It **tastes** a bit **like** chicken.*

Exercise 1

Decide which five sentences are incorrect then correct them.

1. Do you understand? You still look like a bit confused.
2. She said the flight would cost €50 and the hotel €30 a night, which sounds like a really good deal.
3. I had to tell him the bad news. I felt as if terrible afterwards.
4. Don't eat that. It tastes like really disgusting.
5. It's quite frustrating in the class. It sometimes seems as if I'm the only person who wants to study and learn.
6. She sounded like quite upset the last time I spoke to her.
7. I've only met him once, but what he said about women really annoyed me. He seemed like an idiot to me.
8. Do you think this dress makes me look like fat?

DID YOU KNOW?
These verbs are usually used in the simple tense. Sometimes people will use a continuous tense, but the meaning is the same. If in doubt, use the simple tense.
You're looking well! = *You look well.*
I'm feeling a bit ill. = *I feel a bit ill.*

PRESENT SIMPLE AND PRESENT CONTINUOUS

Present simple

We use the present simple to talk about habits / regular repeated activities. We also use the present simple to talk about more permanent things.
*I **train** on Saturdays.* (= a habit / regular repeated activity)
*I **live** in Budapest.* (= this is always true)

We explain 'how often' using adverbs such as *usually, often, sometimes, hardly ever, never*.
*I **usually** play football on Wednesdays.*

Present continuous

We use the present continuous to talk about temporary, unfinished activities.
*She**'s staying** with her brother on the coast.*
*This weather's depressing! It**'s raining** again.*

To emphasise that something is temporary, we often use expressions such as *at the moment, currently, this week* and *this month*.
*I**'m reading** a great book **at the moment**. I'll lend you it when I've finished it.*

We also use the present continuous to talk about things in the future that are already arranged with other people.
*I**'m going** out for dinner with a client **on Friday**.*
*We**'re getting** married in the summer.*

Some verbs are normally used in the simple tense even when the situation is temporary.
*Are you OK? You **seem** a bit sad.*
*I **don't want** to talk about it at the moment. I'm still really upset about it.*

Here are some other verbs like this:

agree	believe	belong	depend	disagree	doubt
forget	hate	know	like	matter	mind
need	owe	own	prefer	realise	sound
seem	suppose	taste	want		

Exercise 1
Choose the correct option.

1. A: What are the hours like where you work?
   B: OK. *I'm usually just working / I usually just work* nine to five, but this month *I'm doing / I do* a lot of extra hours because we've got a really tight deadline to meet, so *I'm starting / I start* at nine in the morning and *finishing / finish* at nine or even ten at night most days.
2. A: Where do you work?
   B: Well, *I'm normally working / I normally work* in the centre of town, but next week *I'm working / I work* from home because they *decorate / are decorating* our office.
3. A: What does your job involve?
   B: It's general office work, really. *I'm answering / I answer* the phone and *making / make* appointments for my boss, that kind of thing, but *we're holding / we hold* a conference in a couple of months, so at the moment *I'm sorting out / I sort out* lots of things for that as well.

Exercise 2
Decide which five sentences are incorrect then correct them.

1. Can you phone back later? I have dinner.
2. Ignore him. He's just being silly.
3. Is she seeing anyone at the moment?
4. I'm annoyed with him. He's still owing me money.
5. I don't need any help thanks. I just look.
6. I go to the shops. Do you want anything?
7. I'm not a tea drinker. I'm preferring coffee.
8. I love cycling. I belong to a local cycling club.

3 TIME OFF

FUTURE PLANS

There is no future tense in English and sometimes there is no real difference in meaning between two forms. Take any explanation of future forms as just a guide, not as fixed rules.

Questions about plans
We use the present continuous or *be going to* + infinitive (without *to*) to ask about plans.
What **are** you **doing** this afternoon?
Are you **going** away in the summer?
Where **are** you **going to stay**?
When **are** you **going to finish** work tonight?
You can also ask:
Do you have any plans for today / this afternoon / the summer?

DID YOU KNOW?
Instead of saying *be going to go*, we often just say *be going*. It's shorter and easier to say. For example, we usually prefer *Are you going away?* to *Are you going to go away?*

Definite plans
We generally prefer to use *be going to* to talk about things that we have decided before we speak. The present continuous is also possible and doesn't change the meaning.
We generally prefer to use the present continuous to talk about arrangements we have made, but we can also use *going to*.
I'm going to travel round Vietnam later in the year.
I'm not going to have a holiday this year.
We're staying in a five-star hotel.
I'm seeing my grandparents on Sunday.
To show the plan or arrangement is an obligation, we use *have to* + infinitive (without *to*).
I have to work long hours in July and August.
I don't have to work on Friday so we could go out then.

Less certain plans
When we have not completely decided a plan or we want to show uncertainty, we use:
will + probably / possibly + infinitive (without *to*)
OR *probably won't* + infinitive (without *to*)
*I'm not absolutely sure, but **I'll probably go** out later.*
*We'**ll possibly go** out later, but it **probably won't be** for long.*
might / may (possibly) (not) + infinitive (without *to*)
*We **might not go** on holiday this year.*
*I **might have to work** right through the summer.*
be thinking of + -ing
A: *I'm **thinking of going** to China. I have a friend there who's invited me to visit. I'll see if I can afford it.*
B: *Really? When **are** you **thinking of going**?*
You may also see the patterns below that show the speaker hasn't fully decided:
It depends ... how much it is / if I have time / on the weather.
I'll see ... what happens / what the weather's like / if I can later.

Exercise 1
Decide if either one or both forms in italics are correct.

1. I can't wait for the holiday. *I have to / I'm going to* see my grandparents in Hong Kong.
2. My dad probably *won't come / isn't coming* with us. It depends how much work he has.
3. Over the holidays, *I have to / I'm having to* study for my exams. It's a pain.
4. We're thinking of *going / to go* to Cuba in April. It's supposed to be great.
5. A: What *are you doing / will you do* in the summer holidays?
   B: I haven't decided really. *I'm going to / I might* just stay at home.
6. A: Do you have any plans *on / for* the weekend?
   B: No, *I'm not doing / I'm not going to do* anything.
7. *I might possibly go / I'm thinking of going* travelling after I finish university. I'll see how much money I have.

will and making decisions
We prefer *be going to* or the present continuous to talk about plans that are certain and exist (i.e. already planned / arranged). However, we prefer *will* when we are making a decision or promise about the future now.
A: *I've just heard I have to go to a meeting later, so I can't drive you to the hospital.*
B: *Don't worry. I'**ll take** the bus instead.*

Exercise 2
Complete the sentences below with the correct form (*will* or *be going to*) of these verbs.

text	be	call	come	see
get	go	visit	do	

1. A: I'm afraid I can't meet you at the station. I _____ in Spain on a work trip that day.
   B: That's OK. I _____ a taxi to my hotel. It's not a problem.
2. A: My plane is landing at around half past six.
   B: OK. Well, I _____ and meet you at the airport, then.
3. A: What are you going to do tomorrow? Do you have any plans?
   B: I _____ a client in the morning, but after that I'm free. I _____ you sometime after one.
4. A: I _____ home now. I'm tired and it's late. I need to sleep.
   B: OK. I _____ you in the meeting tomorrow morning then.
5. A: So what _____ you _____ about it? Any idea?
   B: Hey, my boss is here. Can't talk now. I _____ you back later.

PRESENT PERFECT SIMPLE

The present perfect simple is *have / has* + (*not / never*) + past participle.

I've been to Hiroshima.
He's never been there before.
Have you (ever) **visited** there?

The present perfect simple is used to introduce or list experiences connected to a present discussion.

A: *Do you know where Cologne is?*
B: *Yes. I've actually been there several times.*

A: *Why do you think you'll make a good English teacher?*
B: *Well, I've done some teaching before. I've travelled a lot. I've been to several countries in Europe and Asia, so I think I'll be good at talking to foreign students and I've also tried learning a language myself.*

When we use the present perfect simple, we don't usually say the exact time of the experience.

~~I've been~~ *I went there when I was living in Germany.*
~~I've done~~ *I did some teaching last year.*

Details about the experience are usually in the past simple. We often use a time phrase with these details, but not always.
Well, I've done some teaching before. I taught computer skills to unemployed people back home. I've travelled a lot. I've been to several countries in Europe and Asia. I actually went to Japan a few months ago. So I think I'll be good at talking to foreign students. I've also tried learning a language myself. I tried to learn Japanese before I went there.

Exercise 1
Complete the sentences with the correct form (present perfect simple or past simple) of the verbs.

1 One of the best places I ¹_____ (visit) is Isfahan in Iran. It's a very historic city. About 500 years ago, it ²_____ (be) the capital of Persia. The capital ³_____ (move) to Tehran quite a long time ago, though.

2 I ¹_____ (be) to some great places in my life but, without a doubt, Shanghai is the best. I first ²_____ (go) there in 2002 and I ³_____ (go) back three times since then. It's very different now to how it used to be. In 2002, there ⁴_____ (not / be) as many skyscrapers and not that many people spoke English.

3 I know it sounds strange, but I ¹_____ (be) to Peru five or six times now, but I ²_____ (never / go) outside of Lima, the capital. The last time I ³_____ (be) there, I ⁴_____ (plan) to visit Machu Picchu, but in the end I just ⁵_____ (not / have) time.

4 A: ¹_____ (you / be) to Russia?
  B: Yes, quite a few times. Why?
  A: Well, we're thinking of going there on holiday this summer.
  B: OK. Where to?
  A: Maybe St. Petersburg.
  B: Oh, OK. I ²_____ (only / go) there once and it ³_____ (be) quite a long time ago.
  A: What ⁴_____ (you / think) of it? ⁵_____ (you / like) it?
  B: To be honest, I ⁶_____ (not / see) very much of it. I ⁷_____ (be) only there for a few days. I ⁸_____ (spend) a lot more time in Moscow as my company has an office there.

Answering present perfect questions

When we answer present perfect questions, we often use other tenses. Here are some common answers to the question *Have you ever been to ...?*

Yeah (I have). A couple of times.
 I've been there quite a few times.
 Have you? What did you think of it?
 I went there last year on holiday.
 I went there a few years ago on business.
No (never). I've never really wanted to.
 It's never really appealed to me.
 I've heard it's amazing, though.
 but it's supposed to be great.
 but I'd love to / like to one day.
 but I've always wanted to.
 but I'm going there next month, actually.
 but we're thinking of going there this summer, actually.

Exercise 2
Correct the mistakes in B's answers.

1 A: Have you read *The Shadow of the Wind*?
  B: No, I haven't, but it's supposed to good. Is it?

2 A: Have you discussed the problem with Matt?
  B: Yeah, he's actually rung me about ten minutes ago to talk about it.

3 A: Have you been to that new market yet?
  B: Yes, I have, actually. I've been shopping there yesterday – and guess what? I bumped into Rick while I was there.

4 A: We went to see the musical *We Will Rock You* last night. Have you seen it?
  B: No, but I like to. I've heard it's really good.

5 A: We went to that Italian restaurant round the corner. Have you eaten there yet?
  B: No. What it's like?

6 A: Have you ever done a parachute jump?
  B: No never, but I always want to ever since I was a kid.

7 A: Have you ever been to that fish restaurant on the high street?
  B: Yeah! I went there loads of times. It's one of my favourite restaurants.

8 A: Have you ever been to Seoul?
  B: No, but I'll go there next week.

4 INTERESTS

HABIT AND FREQUENCY

Present and past habits
To talk about present habits, we use adverbs and the present simple.
*I **sometimes go** cycling by the river. It's lovely there.*
*I **never watch** TV. I just don't have time.*

To talk about habits in the past, we use adverbs and the past simple or *used to* + infinitive (without *to*).
*I **hardly ever went** / **used to go** swimming when I was younger.*
*When I was a kid, we **always went** / **used to go** to Blackpool for our summer holidays.*

Asking about frequency
When we ask about frequency of habits, we use these questions:
Do you play tennis much?
Do you go walking a lot?
How often do you do that?
Do you ever go swimming?
Did you go climbing much when you lived in Switzerland?
Did you use to go to that amazing restaurant on the lake?

Grammar reference 89

Answering about frequency

We usually reply to these questions with one of the following phrases and more details.

(Yes / Yeah)   All the time. Maybe three or four times a week.
              A lot. Maybe two or three times a month.
              Quite often / Quite a lot. I probably go once or twice a week.
              Sometimes. It depends how I feel.

(No)   Not that often. I don't have much spare time.
       Hardly ever. The last time I went was about three years ago.
       Never. I'm just not interested.

When we answer a *How often* question, we use a frequency phrase – we don't just say *Yes / No*.
How often do you see your grandmother?
Once a month. / Three times a week.
Once every two months. / Once every three weeks.
Say small numbers first: *once or twice / two or three times*
We also often answer using phrases that compare one thing with another.
Not as much as I used to. (= In the past, I did it more than I do now.)
Not as often as before. (= In the past, I did it more than I do now.)
Not as much as I'd like to. (= I want to do it more, but I can't.)
Not as much as I should. (= I don't do it enough. I feel guilty about it.)
We can also answer questions about frequency with *whenever* meaning 'every time'.
Yes / Yeah. **Whenever** *I can.*
Yes / Yeah. **Whenever** *I get the chance.*
Frequency phrases usually go at the end of sentences.
I go there **once every two or three months**.
I try to visit her **whenever I get the chance**.
She goes running **almost every day**.
Adverbs normally go between the noun and the verb, although they can go in other places.
We **always** *go to that restaurant. Let's go somewhere different.*
In my old job, I **sometimes** *had to work late, but I hardly ever worked weekends.*

Exercise 1

Correct the mistakes with the frequency phrases.

1. A: Do you ever go swimming?
   B: No, hardly never. I don't really like it.
2. A: How often do you go out?
   B: Not much often. I'm very busy with my studies.
3. A: Did you use to go and watch them play a lot?
   B: Yeah, basically once a two weeks.
4. A: Did your parents ever take you to art exhibitions?
   B: Yeah, sometimes. Probably twice or once a year.
5. A: Can we meet on Tuesday evening?
   B: I'm sorry, I can't. Always I go to my art class on Tuesdays.
6. A: So how often do you go walking?
   B: Whenever I will get the chance.
7. A: Do you go to the gym a lot?
   B: Not as much how I should.
8. A: Do you do much sport?
   B: Not as much as I used. I had a foot injury for a while which stopped me.

Exercise 2

Complete the sentences with the correct form of the verbs. There may be more than one possible answer.

1. When I was a kid, my parents _____ me stay out late. (never / let)
2. My brother _____ swimming every morning before I get up. (go)
3. I _____ my parents as much as I used to, now that we've moved. (not / see)
4. When I was at school, I always _____ really hard, but now I'm at university I _____ to. (study, not / need)
5. I _____ an hour in the gym every day, but I hardly ever _____ now. That's why I'm so unfit. (spend, go).

PRESENT PERFECT CONTINUOUS AND PAST SIMPLE FOR DURATION

Present perfect continuous or simple?

To talk about duration when an activity or situation is still taking place or affecting the present situation, we use the present perfect continuous (*have / has + (not) been + -ing*).
How long **have** *you* **been learning** *English? You speak it very well.*
How long **has** *he* **been working** *here? He doesn't seem to know what to do.*
Aren't you tired? You've been driving all day.

Some verbs, such as *know*, *have* and *belong*, are usually used in the simple form (*have / has + (not) + past participle*) rather than the continuous.
How long **have** *you* **known** *each other?*
They've had that car for years. I'm not surprised it breaks down so often.
Have *you* **belonged** *to the club a long time?*

Past simple

To talk about duration when the activity or situation is finished, we use the past simple.
A: *I ran in a team when I was younger.*
B: *How long* **did** *you* **do** *that?*
A: *About five years, I guess. I* **stopped** *when I started working full-time.*
I **lived** *in Brazil for around ten years before I moved back to the States.*
I **played** *tennis for years until I injured my knee and had to give up.*

since

Since or *ever since* show when a current activity / situation started.
since *1993 / April 10th / last Monday / five years ago*
since *his injury / the election / the start of the season / the wedding*
ever since *I was a kid / I got injured / they won the election / we got married*
We usually use *since* phrases with perfect tenses.
I've been really into martial arts **ever since I went to Japan**.

for

For shows the length / period of time something lasted – whether the activity is finished or not.
for *five minutes / six months etc.*
for *ages / hours / weeks / years etc.*
for *a while / a long time / a week etc.*

DID YOU KNOW?

In spoken English, we sometimes miss out *for*, especially in answers to *How long ...?* questions.

A: **How long** have you been waiting?
B: *Half an hour. / Ages.*
I worked there (for) a long time before I got to know people.

Exercise 1

Choose the correct option.

1. A: I have my yoga class tonight.
   B: Really? How long *have you been doing / did you do* that?
2. A: I think I spent too long in the gym yesterday. I'm really stiff this morning.
   B: How long *have you been / were you* there for?
3. A: My brother *'s been skiing / skied* ever since I can remember. He's really good.
   B: I'm jealous! *I've been going / I went* skiing for two weeks once and I never really managed to go more than 100 metres without falling down.
4. A: Are you still going to karate classes?
   B: Yeah, but I have an injury at the moment, so I *haven't been going / didn't go* for a few weeks.
5. A: How long have you been going running?
   B: *Since / For* last year. I feel so much fitter.
6. A: Do you know anyone who'd like to play handball? We *haven't had / haven't been having* enough players *since / for* the end of last season.
   B: You said. I've been trying to persuade my friend to play for you *since / for* ages, but he says he can't commit to playing every week.
   A: Well, he doesn't have to play every week. Once every two weeks would help.

COMMON MISTAKES

1. *You speak German very well. How long* ~~are you~~ **have you been living** *here?*
   Don't use the present continuous (or simple) to talk about the duration of an activity that started in the past but is still taking place or affecting the present situation. Use the present perfect continuous (or simple).
2. *I haven't had any work* ~~from~~ **since** *leaving my last job.*
   I went to university ~~since~~ **from** *2010 till 2014.*
   Use *since* not *from* when talking about the start of a period of time that continues up to now. Use *from / from when* to talk about the start of a period of time which is finished before now.
3. *I waited for the plane* ~~during~~ **for** *two hours and they told us it was cancelled.*
   Don't use *during* to show how long something continued – use *for*. *During* is used to refer to a point within a period of time.
   They only had two shots **during** *the whole match.*

Exercise 2

Correct the mistake in each sentence.

1. I've been doing these exercises during three years. I usually do them for an hour a day.
2. From the accident, it has taken a long time to recover my confidence.
3. I'm studying Chinese for six years now, but I can still only have very basic conversations.
4. My grandparents have been married since fifty years and apparently they've never argued once.
5. I banged my head during the game and I've been having a headache since then.

5 WORKING LIFE

MUST AND *CAN'T* FOR COMMENTING

We often use *must* or *can't* + infinitive (without *to*) when we comment on other people's experiences. This shows we are guessing about things, though we think we are probably right.

A: *I'm a heart surgeon.*
B: *Really? Wow! That* **must be** *stressful.* (= I'm guessing this is true, but I understand your experience may be different and I may be wrong.)

We use *must* in positive sentences. In negative sentences, we use *can't*.

A: *I've been working here for ten years now.*
B: *Wow. So you* **must enjoy** *it.*
A: *My husband is ill and off work at the moment, so I'm working full-time and looking after the kids.*
B: *Oh! That* **can't be** *easy.*

Responding to *must / can't* comments

When we reply to *must / can't* comments, we usually use a present (or past) tense to show the true facts or our own true feelings / experiences. We may use a form of the auxiliary verb *be* to avoid repeating an adjective or a form of the auxiliary verb *do* to avoid repeating a verb.

A: *It must be difficult.*
B: *Yes, it* **is** *(difficult).*
B: *It* **is** *(difficult) sometimes.*
B: *No, not really. / Actually it* **isn't** *(difficult).*

A: *It can't be easy.*
B: *No, it* **isn't** *(easy).*
B: *Oh, it* **'s** *OK.*
A: *Actually, it* **is** *(easy).*

A: *You must enjoy it.*
B: *Yeah, I* **do** *(enjoy it).*
B: *I* **do** *(enjoy it) most of the time.*
B: *Not really. / Actually I* **don't** *(enjoy it).*

A: *You can't enjoy it that much.*
B: *No, I* **don't** *(enjoy it very much).*
B: *Well, I* **do** *sometimes (enjoy it).*
B: *Actually I* **do** *(enjoy it).*

Must is much more commonly used to comment on other people's experiences and feelings than *can't*, so practise *must* comments and replies more.

Exercise 1

Complete the dialogues with one word in each space. Contractions count as one word.

1. A: We're so busy. I think I've worked 70 hours this week.
   B: Wow. You _____ be exhausted.
   A: I _____ , but it's going to be the same next week too.
2. A: Between emergencies, we often have nothing to do for hours.
   B: You _____ get quite bored.
   A: Yeah, we _____ sometimes, but I read a lot and we sometimes play cards.
3. A: My husband is away a lot with work.
   B: That _____ be easy when you have three young kids.
   A: _____ , it's fine. My mother helps me.
4. A: The chemicals we use have a very strong smell.
   B: That must _____ horrible.
   A: _____ really. I mean, it _____ to begin with, but you quickly get used to it.
5. A: The kids just don't listen.
   B: You must _____ to scream at them sometimes. I know I would.
   A: I do! But obviously I _____ actually do it. Shouting doesn't work.

Grammar reference 91

We can also follow *must / can't* with *be + -ing* to form a present continuous meaning, and *have been* when talking about the past.

A: *They're going to give me a bonus.*
B: *You* ~~*are doing well*~~ **must be doing** *well.*
A: *Yes, I am.*

A: *They were two hours late.*
B: *You* ~~*were*~~ **must've been** *annoyed.*
A: *Yeah, I was. Really annoyed.*

DID YOU KNOW?
We sometimes use *I bet* instead of *must / can't*. For example, in Exercise 1, we could say:
I bet *you're exhausted.*
I bet *you get quite bored.*
I bet *that isn't good.*

Exercise 2
Rewrite these responses using *I bet*.

1	He must've been furious.	I bet he _____ .
2	They can't be making any money.	I bet they _____ .
3	That can't be very interesting.	I bet that _____ .
4	He must be earning good money.	I bet he _____ .
5	She can't have been feeling well.	I bet she _____ .
6	That can't have been much fun.	I bet that _____ .
7	You must be pleased about that.	I bet you _____ .
8	You must've been driving too fast.	I bet you _____ .

TALKING ABOUT RULES

must / mustn't
We sometimes use *must(n't)* + infinitive (without *to*) to show it's essential (not) to do something, especially when you made the rule and / or have authority.
You **must arrive** *in class on time. I don't allow any students in the class if they are late.*
You **mustn't use** *these computers for personal use.*
Must(n't) sounds very strong so we usually replace it with other structures.

have to and be supposed to
We usually use *have to* + infinitive (without *to*) instead of *must* as it sounds less direct and rude. We also use it to ask about rules.
I **have to wear** *a stupid uniform at work. I hate it!*
Do *I* **have to attend** *all the staff meetings?*
We also use *be supposed to* + infinitive (without *to*) to replace *must*, especially where a rule has just been broken or is often not followed.
I'm **supposed to be** *available to cover if anyone is off sick.*
*Hey, don't leave your dirty cup in the sink! You***'re supposed to wash** *them yourself.*

can't, be not allowed to, be not supposed to
We usually use *can't* or *be not allowed to* + infinitive (without *to*) instead of *mustn't*. They mean it's not possible to do something.
We **can't work** *from home in my company.*
*Sorry, but you***'re not allowed to bring** *dogs in here.*
We also use *be not supposed to* + infinitive (without *to*) to replace *mustn't*, especially where the rule has just been broken or is often not followed.
*You***'re not supposed to use** *this entrance into the building, but it's more convenient.*

can, be allowed to
We use *can* or *be allowed to* + infinitive (without *to*) to ask about rules, to show there is no rule or to say that a rule says it is OK to do something.
Can *I* **use** *any of the computers in the building?*
Are *we* **allowed to work** *from home at all?*
We **are allowed to start** *work late if we then work later in the evening to make up the time.*

Exercise 1
Choose the correct option.

1. Sorry, *you're not allowed to / you have to* smoke in here. Can you go outside please?
2. *Are you allowed to / Are you supposed to* wear jeans at work? I don't really have anything else to wear!
3. *I'm supposed to / I can* carry my ID at all times, but nobody ever asks me for it!
4. *Do you have to / Can you* ask your manager if you want to leave the office?
5. *We are allowed to / aren't supposed to* come out here on the roof of the building, but it's a really nice place to have a break!
6. *You can't / You're not really supposed to* eat or drink in the classroom, so please tidy everything up after you finish your coffee.
7. *We have to / are allowed to* belong to a trade union, but not many people are members.
8. *I can't / have to* start really early some days, but at least *I have to / I'm allowed to* go home early.

DID YOU KNOW?
A more formal word you may see written is *permitted*.
Smoking **is only permitted** *outside.* (= allowed)

Exercise 2
Complete the second sentence so that it has a similar meaning to the first sentence using the word given. Do not change the word given. You must use between three and five words, including the word given.

1. You shouldn't really leave before five, but there's nothing to do now.
   SUPPOSED
   I know you _____ before five, but there's nothing to do now.
2. We're not allowed to give out personal details of clients.
   PERMITTED
   Giving out personal details of clients _____ .
3. You absolutely mustn't make any noise while the exam is taking place.
   HAVE
   We _____ really quiet while the exam is taking place.
4. There's a room at the back of the building where you can smoke.
   ONLY
   You're _____ in the room at the back of the building.
5. It's against company rules to leave your computer on overnight.
   OFF
   You _____ your computer when you go home. It's a company rule.
6. Don't tell anyone I'm here. I told everyone else I'm working from home.
   SUPPOSED
   _____ working from home, so don't tell anyone I'm here.

6 BUYING AND SELLING

COMPARISONS

Comparative adjectives
To make comparative adjectives we add *-er* to adjectives of one syllable.
Two-syllable adjectives ending in *-y* change to *-ier*.
We use *more* with two or three-syllable words.
A: *This one is **cheaper**.*
B: *Yes, but this one is **easier** to navigate and the camera is **more powerful**.*
Remember that some comparative forms are irregular, e.g. *good – better*, *bad – worse*.
Often we don't mention both things we are comparing because it's obvious. However, when we compare two things in the same sentence, we use *than*.
*I'm with Blue. They're **cheaper than** the other companies.*

Big and small differences
To say there's a big difference, add *much, way, far, a lot, quite a lot* before the comparative adjective.
To say there's a small difference, add *a bit, slightly, a little bit*.

Negative comparisons
To make negative comparisons, we can use *not as … as*.
*It looks nice, but it's **not as fast as** the other tablet we looked at.*
*Their selection **isn't as varied as** it used to be in the past.*
Note that *as … as* means two things are equal or the same.
*My phone is **as good as** yours.*
We can also use *less* to make negative comparisons before any adjective.
*It looks nice, but it's **less fast**.*
*Their selection is **less varied than** it used to be in the past.*

twice / three times, etc.
We sometimes make comparisons using *twice / three times / half*, etc. The two patterns are:
twice as + adjective + *as*
twice the + noun + *of*
*It's not cheap. It's about **twice as expensive as** the phone you have now.*
*It's a lot cheaper than the other one we looked at, but then it's almost **half as powerful**.*
*Their new place is almost **three times the size of** their old flat.*
*It is a bit better, but it's more than **twice the price**. I don't think it's worth it.*

Exercise 1
Complete the sentences with the correct form of the adjectives. Then underline the adjectives and the words used before them to show the size of the difference. The first one is done for you.

1 This phone looks <u>much nicer</u>, but the problem is, the battery doesn't last nearly _____ . (nice, long)
2 These speakers are quite a lot _____ so the sound quality on them is far _____ . (big, good)
3 This one is a lot _____ , but it's probably worth it. It's not _____ the other phones, so it's much _____ to carry. (expensive, heavy, easy)
4 I know it's not _____ the other phones on the market, but I'm really into photography, and the camera on this one takes much _____ quality photos. (cheap, high)
5 To be honest, for me, the brand name is a lot less _____ the speed it operates at. (important)

6 If the screen is a bit _____ , then usually it's slightly _____ to navigate and it's not _____ to see all the icons and everything. (large, easy, difficult)
7 It is lovely, but it's also way _____ the phone I have at the moment. (expensive)
8 Personally, I'd rather have a phone that wasn't _____ and was slightly _____ if it meant I also had a _____ battery that lasted longer. (thin, heavy, efficient)

Exercise 2
Complete the second sentence with an adjective and other words so that it has a similar meaning to the first sentence.

1 The screen on this one is twice the size of the one you have at the moment.
   The screen on this one is twice _____ the one you have at the moment.
2 My old phone was almost double the weight of this new one.
   My old phone was almost twice _____ this new one.
3 My old deal was twice the price of my current one.
   My old deal was twice _____ my current one.
4 The connection here is terrible. It's half the speed of my one at home.
   The connection here is terrible. It's twice _____ my one at home.
5 The business has really grown since last year. We have three times the work.
   The business has really grown since last year. We are three times _____ .

NOUN PHRASES

Compound nouns (noun + noun)
Compound nouns are formed by adding two nouns together. The first noun describes the main noun. The first noun is like an adjective and is not made plural.
a silk scarf / silk scarves (= scarves which are made out of silk)
a paperweight / paperweights (= a weight for holding down paper)

Noun + 's / s'
We use noun + *'s* to show a particular thing belongs to a particular person, animal or organisation. If a particular thing belongs to more than one person, animal or organisation, we use noun + *s'*. We usually use noun + noun to talk about general connections between other things.
***My wife's student** / **my wife's students** gave her a lovely present.*
*It's **my parents' wedding anniversary** next month.* (It's the anniversary of both of my parents.)
***The hotel's** restaurant was very good.* (The restaurant belonging to one particular hotel.)
***Hotel restaurants** are usually very expensive.* (All restaurants in different hotels.)

Adjective order
The most important rule about adjective order is that opinions go before facts. Nouns always go next to the main noun.
*a **horrible yellow** tie.*   (*horrible* is an opinion)
*a **yellow silk** tie*   (*silk* is a noun)
*a **lovely big** bunch of flowers* (*lovely* is more of an opinion than *big*)
We usually only use one or two adjectives before a noun. We hardly ever use more than three.

Grammar reference 93

Prepositional phrases

We can add information after nouns using phrases beginning with different prepositions.

We use *with* to show a feature of the main noun.

*a tie **with** a picture / a shirt **with** horrible buttons / a guy **with** black hair*

We use *of* to explain the specific thing you see on the main noun or what it contains.

*a postcard **of** the Niagara Falls / a model **of** the Eiffel Tower / a bottle **of** water*

We use *from* to show where the main noun was made or where you met a person.

*some cheese **from** Norway / a shirt **from** Bolivia / a friend **from** university*

We use *for + -ing* to show the purpose of the main noun.

*a pan **for** cooking paella / a machine **for** making coffee*

We use a variety of different prepositions to show the position of an object.

*the photos **on** the shelf / a box **under** the stairs / the drawer **in** my bedroom*

Exercise 1
Choose the correct option.

1 He said they were made from genuine *cow leather / leather cows*, but they were so cheap, I'm not sure I believe him.
2 I wanted to buy this *beautiful Turkish rug / Turkish beautiful rug*, but I couldn't afford it.
3 They bought us some wine *from / with* their region as a present. I didn't tell them we don't drink!
4 My second *wife's son / son's wife* is pregnant, so I'm going to become a grandfather.
5 I bought *Real Madrid's shirt / a Real Madrid shirt* for my son.
6 I bought this huge pan *for / with* cooking this rice dish they make called *plov*. It was a nightmare to bring it home on the plane!
7 They sell a lot of *plastic tacky toys / tacky plastic toys* in the *market street / street market* in the main square.
8 He was wearing a top *with / of* a picture *from / of* Mickey Mouse.

Exercise 2
Decide which six sentences are incorrect then correct them.

1 I want to get one of those fridge magnets to take home for my flat.
2 I need to buy presents for both my sister's weddings this summer!
3 I found this amazing stuff for to keep leather shoes in good condition.
4 My son bought me an Italian beautiful silk tie for my birthday.
5 I'm looking after the house of my parents this week. They're away on holiday.
6 You should buy some cheese of this area to take home with you.
7 My girlfriend bought me this awful comedy tie with a cartoon of Superman in it.
8 I need to buy a couple of wool scarves for the winter.

7 EDUCATION

FUTURE TIME CLAUSES

To specify the time at which a future action will happen, we often use a clause starting with a time expression such as the following:

(right) after   the moment
as soon as   until
before   when
once   while

Present tenses, future meaning

The verbs in the clauses after the time expressions always use a present tense to refer to a future situation or action. This can be the present simple or the present perfect. The present perfect emphasises that the action / situation happened before the point in the future. Don't use *will* or *going to*.

*I'll tell him the news **when** he ~~will get~~ **gets** home.*
*We'll start cooking **as soon as** the kids ~~are going to get back~~ **have got back** from school.*

We can also begin sentences with the time clauses. It depends whether we want to emphasise the action or the time the action will happen at.

***The moment** he **comes** through the door, I'll tell him to call you.*
***Once** I've **finished** this bit, I'll come and help you with that, OK?*

Exercise 1
Rewrite each pair of sentences as one sentence.

1 I'm going to leave school next month. Then I might go away for a few weeks.
   After _____ , I _____ .
2 The course finishes soon. Then I'll have to start paying back all my debts.
   Once _____ , I _____ .
3 You're going to move to Germany soon. Are you going to look for a job there?
   Are _____ when _____ ?
4 I have my final exams soon. I'm not going to go out.
   I _____ until _____ .
5 I'm in a lecture at the moment. It finishes at three. Then I'll call you back.
   I _____ right after _____ .
6 He's going to graduate next year. He said he's immediately going to burn all his notes.
   He said he _____ the moment _____ .
7 I'm waiting to hear from my boss. I promise I'll call you right after he calls me, OK?
   I _____ you as soon as I _____ .
8 I start university in September. I'll need to work part-time to help pay for everything.
   I start university in September. I'll need to _____ while I _____ to help pay for everything.
9 I graduate next spring, but I think I'll need to start looking for a job before then.
   I _____ a job before I _____ in the spring.

Future possibilities and certainties

Where the future situation is only a possibility and not a certainty, we use *if*.

*I'm not sure I'll have time, but ~~when~~ **if I do**, I'll do the shopping later.*
***If / When I pass**, my dad's going to buy me a car. (Both are possible – it depends how confident you are!)*
*Give this letter to your mum ~~if~~ **when you get home from school**. It's urgent.*
*~~If~~ **When I die**, my children will get everything I own.*

Instead of *if*, we sometimes use *as long as*.

*I'll help you study for your exams **as long as** you help me improve my English.*

94

Exercise 2
Choose the correct option.
1. I'll phone you *when / if* I can't come to the meeting.
2. After I *will finish / finish* my Master's, I'm going to do a PhD.
3. I'll phone you *when / if* I get home.
4. I'm going to have a holiday *once / if* my final exams have finished. I deserve it!
5. I'm going to take a nice, long holiday once the course *finished / has finished*.
6. If you're strict with them, you'll gain their respect – *as soon as / as long as* you're fair as well.
7. I'm probably going to Canada to study English before I *will start / start* university.
8. I'm going to bed *as soon as / if* I get to the hotel.

ZERO AND FIRST CONDITIONALS
Regular situations
We can use the zero conditional to talk about situations that regularly happen or rules. The *if*-clause and the result clause are both in a present tense. We can replace *if* with *when* in these sentences. There's no difference in meaning.

	regular situation (*if*-clause)	result clause
regular situation	*If I try* to explain something,	they *sit* whispering to each other.
rule	*If* a child *skips* school	the parents *can be fined*.

Possible future situations
To discuss possible future situations we use *if* + a present tense. To discuss the results of that situation you can use *will* or *going to* for results you think are definite and *might* for results you think are possible. This is called a first conditional.

	possible future situation (*if*-clause)	result clause
will / going to = definitely	*If* they *don't accept* me,	I'll *retake* / I'm *going to retake* the test.
might = less certain	*If* they *don't accept* me,	I *might look* for another Master's.
won't = definitely not	*If* you *don't produce* a doctor's certificate,	we *won't accept* any excuses to do with illness.

Advice
We can also use a conditional to offer advice about a possible future situation.

	possible future situation (*if*-clause)	result clause
imperative	*If* they *talk*,	*send* them to the headteacher.
should	*If* you *have* any problems,	you *should* contact the student counselling service.

unless
We use *unless* to mean 'if not'.
We won't accept any excuses to do with illness **unless** you produce a doctor's certificate.
He'll probably fail, **unless** he starts studying a bit harder.
Don't speak **unless** I tell you to.

DID YOU KNOW?
We only use a comma when the *if*-clause comes first.
You won't gain the students' respect **if** you're not strict.
If you're not strict, you won't gain the students' respect.

Exercise 1
Choose the correct option.
1. Next time, just ask if you *need / will need* to borrow my notes.
2. I *might / should* skip the lecture tomorrow if I'm still feeling tired.
3. I'm a bit stressed because if I *fail / will fail* this module, I fail the whole course.
4. I usually find if I don't revise my notes straight after class, I *forget / will forget* most of it.
5. If you're finding the course difficult, *tell / you will tell* your teacher.
6. My tutor's quite strict if you *are not working / might not work* hard enough.
7. He's so annoying. If I tell him to be quiet, he always *will ignore / ignores* me.
8. I got good marks on my coursework so I'll definitely pass *if / unless* I mess up the exam really badly.

Exercise 2
Decide which six sentences are incorrect then correct them.
1. If you want to get a good grade, you'll have to work a lot harder!
2. If he'll find a job, he might move out.
3. They told us that if he skips any more classes, they're going to ask him to leave the course.
4. Your students don't behave better if you don't set some clear rules.
5. What you will do if you don't get offered a place on a Master's?
6. I won't can finish this essay by tomorrow unless you give me some peace and quiet!
7. You'll fail the exam if you revise properly.
8. If you won't have your passport or some other kind of ID, they'll refuse to register you on the course.

8 EATING

GENERALISATIONS AND *TEND TO*
We can show that something is generally true by using *tend to*, adverbial phrases or adverbs.

tend to
Tend to + infinitive (without *to*) can be used in different tenses as with normal verbs.
I **tend to avoid** red meat if I can. I **tend to** mainly **eat** vegetables, rice and fish.
We generally didn't go out much at night. We **tended to eat** in the hotel.
Since I saw that documentary about factory farming, **I've tended to avoid** eating chicken.
The negative form is normally *tend not to*. However, *don't tend to* is also possible.
I **tend not to eat** after seven at night.
I **don't tend to eat** after seven at night.
We **tended not to eat** much meat when I was younger because it was so expensive.

Adverbial phrases

We can use the following adverbial phrases to mean *generally / tend to*. They go at the beginning of the sentence or clause.
In general, people here don't eat much foreign food.
On the whole, people meet in a restaurant rather than at their home.
As a rule, we didn't eat much meat when I was a kid.
Generally speaking, I eat after seven at night.

Adverbs

You can also use adverbs like *usually*, *generally*, *normally* or *hardly ever / any*. They usually go between the subject and the verb.
I **normally** stay at home during the week.
People **hardly ever** kiss in public.

In negative sentences, they usually come after the auxiliary verb and before the main verb.
I don't **normally** eat lunch.
People don't **generally** kiss in public.

Exercise 1

Complete the sentences with one word in each space. Contractions count as one word.

1 I don't like cooking, so I _____ to eat out a lot.
2 _____ general, the food here is really good.
3 I don't _____ eat shellfish, but this is really nice.
4 People here _____ complain if the service is bad. It's just that I personally tend _____ to.
5 As a _____ , I eat as healthily as I can, so I _____ ever eat fried foods.
6 The problem is, most people _____ tend to think about where meat comes from once it's packaged, so _____ speaking, they don't worry that much about animal welfare.
7 On the _____ , food from my country is fairly unhealthy, but I still love it.
8 He has a terrible diet. I mean, he eats hardly _____ vegetables or fruit.

SECOND CONDITIONALS

We use second conditionals to speculate about situations and possible results. They usually have two parts: an *if*-clause referring to the situation and a second clause showing results or consequences.

We use the past simple, past continuous (or *could*) in the *if*-clause. The *if*-clause refers to a situation in the present or future which is impossible to change or is not going to take place.

The other clause explains the imagined results or consequences. We use *would* + infinitive (without *to*) to show a definite result, or *might* + infinitive (without *to*) to show a possible result.

Either clause can come first. When the *if*-clause comes first, add a comma after it.
If I **ate** this kind of thing every day, **I'd get** really fat!
If I **wasn't working** part-time in the restaurant, **I wouldn't be able to pay** my university fees.
I'd go there more often **if** it **wasn't** so expensive!
It'd be better **if** they **served** bigger portions.
You're so unadventurous! **If** you actually **tried** it, you **might like** it!
I'd buy more organic food **if** it **was** / **were** cheaper.
If it **wasn't** / **weren't** so expensive, **I'd shop** there all the time.

DID YOU KNOW?
It is very common in spoken English to say *If I / he / she / it was ...* . However, some people see this as incorrect and prefer *If I / he / she / it were ...* .

Exercise 1

Choose the correct option.

1 I'd love to come tonight, but I'm afraid I have to take an important client out to dinner. If it *is / was / would be* anyone else, I *cancel / will cancel / would cancel* it, but I really can't. Sorry.
2 It's not really my kind of place, to be honest. Perhaps if I *am / would be / were* a bit younger, I *enjoy / might enjoy / would be enjoy* it, but it's just a bit too trendy for me now.
3 That sounds horrible! I don't know what I *do / would do / will do* if that *happens / would happen / happened* to me.
4 I *would be / am / will be* happy to have the party at our place if our flat *is / were / would be* a bit bigger, but it's just too small for something like this.
5 It's a lovely place, but it's not cheap! I mean, you *will only go / would only go / only go* there if you *would be / will be / were* earning good money!

Exercise 2

Decide which six sentences are incorrect then correct them.

1 I will really miss eating fried chicken if I were a vegetarian!
2 You'd be in trouble if you had to use chopsticks all the time!
3 I wouldn't eat tripe even if you'd pay me!
4 You might lose weight if you didn't drink so much!
5 They would can make more money if they started stocking more foreign food.
6 If I would be better at cooking, I might invite people round for dinner more often.
7 I'd be happy to pay for dinner sometimes – if you wanted me to!
8 I would go crazy if I had to go on a diet!
9 I wouldn't ask you if I wouldn't really need your help.
10 If I am you, I'd just do what it tells you to do in the book.

INFORMATION FILES

FILE 1

Unit 1 page 9   CONVERSATION PRACTICE

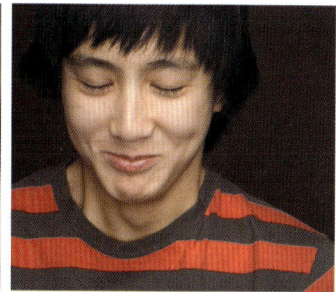

FILE 2

Unit 3 page 30   READING

STRANGE WORLD   LUCY CLEGG

As you can probably tell, **my initial reaction when I first** read about the phenomenon of disaster tourism and experiences **was to** think these people are mad. I saw it as holidays in other people's misery. **I told myself that there's no way** I would be interested in anything like that, but then I started thinking about some of the places I've visited over the years. I slowly came to realise that maybe I'm not so different. For instance, I've been to the Hiroshima Peace Memorial Park, **which commemorates the people who died** as a result of the first nuclear bomb. I've visited many castles, like the Tower of London, where people were executed. Last year I went to Pompeii, the ancient ruins of a city **which was completely destroyed by** a volcano in the first century. While there, I took a photo of a 2,000-year-old dead person. OK, I didn't take a smiling photo of myself in front of it, like the people on the website 'Selfies at serious places'. But still, **looking at** it **now, I am wondering** why I took it and I've come to the conclusion that perhaps I am a disaster tourist myself.

I guess I go to these places because I'm interested in history. Visiting them reminds you of the power of nature and the value of your life. Many so-called disaster tourists actually have similar motivations, it's just that the 'history' is now. Nicholas Wood of the company Political Tours says: 'We're not for people looking for danger, we're for people who want a deeper understanding of the world.' His company sometimes takes clients to scenes of recent conflict to meet local people and experts, but may equally help clients understand the risks of the globalised financial world by touring the City of London and introducing them to decision-makers there.

James Wilcox, whose company does specialise in active areas of conflict, also argues his 'disaster' tours bring much-needed money to the places affected and locals welcome them. 'To be honest, the majority think we're crazy, but the second reaction is they're proud. It's as if they've almost forgotten they **have a lot to offer**. They might be struggling, but other people are **willing to take the risk and** travel halfway around the world to visit.'

Maybe disaster tourism isn't such a disaster.

Information files 97

FILE 3

Unit 2 page 21 SPEAKING

Student A

You bump into someone you knew at school. You stop to say 'hello' and you are really happy to see them again. When you were at school, you had difficulties with schoolwork and with other students, but you always liked this person. Now you are very successful.

- Think about what you do now and your situation – for example, work, family, etc. (This can be true or you can invent the information.)
- Try to keep the conversation going for as long as you can, even if the other person tries to end it.
- Offer to meet or take them out somewhere in the future – think about where and when.
- Remember, you don't want to lose touch again.

FILE 4

Unit 6 page 53 CONVERSATION PRACTICE

Student A

You are a customer. Decide:

- how much you currently pay for your phone.
- how many text messages you get per month: 200? 400? 500?
- how many minutes you get per month: 300? 500? 800?
- Then decide what questions you want to ask about the new phone:
  - camera?
  - battery life?
  - screen size?
  - how well does the operating system link with other devices?
  - how easy is it to navigate?

FILE 5

Unit 7 page 63 CONVERSATION PRACTICE

Student A

- You are studying Medicine. It's a five-year course. Decide which year you are in.
- You have an exam on endocrine systems. Use a dictionary so you can explain it.
- You are positive about the course, your tutors and classmates. Think of reasons why.
- You want to become a doctor.
- You are going to talk to a friend who is studying Business Management.

FILE 6

Unit 7 page 66 READING

Student A

Hattie gives a score for the effectiveness of each factor. Anything with a negative score has a negative effect. 0 has no effect. 0.4 is the average positive effect.

Teachers having high levels of subject knowledge   Score: 0.09

The level of qualifications that teachers have in their subject doesn't have very much impact. This may be because in many classes the level of knowledge the students are learning is quite low, for example primary school maths. What's more important is the teacher's ability to be clear, encouraging and good at giving feedback.

Programmes to extend students' vocabulary   Score: 0.67

Trying to increase the amount of vocabulary students know seems to work well, especially providing both definitions and examples of how the words are used. It's an example of challenging students and helps with several subjects by improving reading skills.

Setting up schools outside of government control   Score: 0.2

Several countries have set up schools (e.g. Charter schools in the USA) which are more independent from government: they can choose what to teach, which teachers to employ, etc. They get some money from the government and some from private sources so students don't have to pay. They do make a difference, but just a very small one.

FILE 7

Unit 2 page 21 **SPEAKING**

Student B

Someone you knew from school stops you outside a shopping mall. You hardly recognise them. They had struggled at school. They weren't very popular, although you got on quite well. Now they look different, are very well dressed and seem to be very successful.

- Think about what your situation is – for example, work, family, etc. (This can be true or you can invent the information.)
- Have a conversation with them for five minutes.
- You are in a bit of a rush so you will try to end the conversation – think of a reason.
- Although you liked them, your life is very busy and you don't need a new friend. Try to avoid making any arrangements in the future – think of excuses.

FILE 8

Unit 6 page 53 **CONVERSATION PRACTICE**

Student B

You are a salesperson in a mobile phone shop. Think about the phone you want to sell.

- Decide the details of the phone:
  - camera?
  - battery life?
  - screen size?
  - links with other devices?
  - user experience?
- What makes it better than other phones?
  - battery?
  - price?
  - something else?
- How many text messages per month you can offer: 200? 400? 500?
- How many minutes per month you can offer: 300? 500? 800?
- What price can you offer?

FILE 9

Unit 6 page 54 **READING**

Shop till you drop!

Add up your score:
A answers = 1   B answers = 3   C answers = 5

14–28
You really can't stand shopping. Some people might even say you're mean because you never spend money, although you prefer to say it's because of political reasons such as protecting the environment. Fashion doesn't interest you and sometimes people say you look scruffy or old-fashioned. You're only interested in getting the cheapest things available.

29–42
You don't mind shopping, but you're quite careful with your money and you often keep an eye out for bargains. You want to look good, but you also want clothes to last, so the latest fashions don't interest you so much. There's more to life than shopping.

43–56
You're quite fashion conscious and love shopping. It's one of your main leisure activities and it often cheers you up. You probably have a particular obsession – shoes, shirts, DVDs. Although you generally control your spending, from time to time you spend more than you should. Sometimes you buy things without thinking and then later realise it was a bad idea.

57–70
Your only interest is shopping and fashion and you are out of control! You can't go shopping without buying something – even if you don't need it. You follow all the latest fashions and have drawers and wardrobes full of clothes you hardly ever wear. Your buying habits are getting you into debt. You should get some help before you end up owing the bank too much money!

FILE 10

Unit 7 page 63   CONVERSATION PRACTICE

Student B

You are studying Business Management.

- One of your current modules is Tax and Accounting. Use a dictionary so you can explain it.
- You're struggling. Think of reasons why.
- The tutors are not so good. Think of reasons why.
- You want to get a job in a bank.
- You are going to talk to a friend who is studying Medicine.

FILE 12

Unit 7 page 66   READING

Student B

Hattie gives a score for the effectiveness of each factor. Anything with a negative score has a negative effect. 0 has no effect. 0.4 is the average positive effect.

Reducing class sizes by 50%   Score: 0.21

Smaller classes are better, but the increase in achievement is very small. Hattie suggests that one reason for this may be that teachers don't change the way they teach when the class size is reduced.

Provide information on how students will be assessed and feedback on what they did   Score: 0.73

This has a very positive effect. Hattie says it is because students will often try harder when it is clear how they can get a higher grade. If the teacher then shows the next steps to improve, this is more encouraging than saying just 'well done'.

Talking about students' expectations   Score: 1.44

This had the highest effect in Hattie's study. When you ask students to grade themselves or to predict their grades in exams (sometimes called 'self-report grades'), they are often very accurate. Hattie suggests this is because they have learnt what level they are by what teachers say or how they are grouped in class. By asking students, teachers understand their expectations better, and can then challenge their students and show them how to exceed these expectations.

FILE 13

Unit 7 page 66 **READING**

Student C

Hattie gives a score for the effectiveness of each factor. Anything with a negative score has a negative effect. 0 has no effect. 0.4 is the average positive effect.

Practising what you have learnt over time   Score: 0.71

Sometimes people learn something then immediately practise it. They might do several practice activities in the same short space of time. However, the evidence from Hattie's research is that it is much better to do some learning, then leave it; practise a day or so later, then leave it; then practise again a week later, etc. This is called 'Spaced Practice'.

Doing homework   Score: 0.29

Students everywhere might be happy to hear that homework isn't very effective. However, Hattie says it depends at what age and what kind. In primary school, it has no effect at all (nearly 0). In secondary school, the effect is higher (nearer 0.4), especially if it is a simple, short practice of what has been learnt (see practice over time). He doesn't recommend *not* giving it!

Summer holidays   Score: –0.09

There are complaints that long summer holidays are bad for student achievement, and unfortunately if you are a student or teacher it is true! However, the negative effect is very small so maybe there are other things we should worry about first!

FILE 14

Unit 8 page 70 **VOCABULARY**

1. olives
2. oysters
3. raisins
4. squid
5. prawns
6. corn on the cob
7. peanuts
8. limes
9. kebabs
10. spinach
11. trifle
12. tripe
13. blue cheese
14. radishes

Information files 101

FILE 15

Unit 8 page 72 **READING**

Student B

YA-WEN (Taiwanese)

I work for a big accounting firm and they transferred me to the States a couple of years ago. It's been quite a shock! For one thing, the portions here tend to be enormous. You see people with steaks the size of their plate – and they eat it all! It's really off-putting. Even worse is steak with blue cheese sauce. I can't stand the way it smells! Why would you put something which is basically mouldy cow fat in your mouth? And it's served with French fries all the time! I really miss having rice with my meals.

Of course there's good food here too. To begin with, there are some good Taiwanese restaurants here! There are also lots of amazing health food shops. I've also got some friends who are great cooks and they often have me round for dinner. Back home, we tend to meet in restaurants, so it's a lovely thing to do.

One last thing that I sometimes find frustrating is the way people usually order things individually for themselves. Sometimes you choose something which doesn't turn out to be that nice and the food goes to waste. It would be better if people shared more. That way, everyone would get something they like.

ALAN (Scottish)

One of the first things I saw when I came to Valencia to teach English was people pouring oil on their bread. I thought it was really weird, but then I tried it and I quite like it now. It's not so different to spreading butter on bread.

In general, there's a lot more good food here and people tend to buy fresh food every day and cook, rather than buying lots of ready meals from the supermarket. Eating out is also good. I always enjoy ordering *tapas* – lots of little dishes that you share.

Having said that, it's not very good if you're a vegetarian. A friend of mine came over and they were always giving him 'vegetable' dishes with bits of ham or sausage in them. It's quite strange – they don't seem to think of ham as meat! The other thing is, it's difficult to get food which isn't Spanish – maybe because there's a lot of regional variation. I love curry, but there are hardly any Indian restaurants here and the curry is never spicy enough!

One last thing that I'm still not used to is having dinner so late. When we eat out, we sometimes don't get to the restaurant until around eleven, and I'm usually starving by then!

AUDIO SCRIPTS

UNIT 1

▶ TRACK 1

1

A = Alfie, H = Holly

A: Hi. Nice to meet you. I'm Alfie.
H: Hey. Holly. How's it going?
A: Yeah, OK, thanks. I'm a bit nervous though, to be honest.
H: Yeah? Why?
A: I don't know. You know … first class. New people.
H: Yeah, I remember that feeling. Don't worry. You'll be fine. It'll be fun.
A: So have you studied here before?
H: Yeah, last term.
A: Oh really? OK. And did you enjoy it?
H: Yeah, it was amazing. Our teacher was brilliant. Really great. So patient and helpful, you know. So, what about you? How long've you been learning French?
A: For about three years now, I guess, but just on my own at home, using the Internet.
H: Yeah? Have you learned much?
A: Well, my reading has improved and I've learned quite a lot of vocabulary, but I really need to practise my speaking more, you know. That's why I'm here. What about you? Why are you learning?
H: Well, I'd like to be a translator and French is an official EU language and UN language, so … you know.
A: Wow! OK.

2

N = Noah, G = Giuliana

N: So what did you make of that session?
G: Oh, um. Well, it was … um … different, wasn't it?
N: I'm glad I'm not the only person that didn't really enjoy it.
G: So, what's your name, then? Where are you based?
N: Oh, I'm Noah.
G: Giuliana. Hi.
N: Hey. And I'm originally from Canada, from Halifax, but I'm working in Santiago now.
G: Oh really? Nice. How long have you been there?
N: A couple of years now. Do you know it? Have you been there?
G: Yeah, loads of times. I'm from Mendoza, just the other side of the mountains. We can drive there in five or six hours. Great city.
N: I like it, yes.
G: What are you doing there? Are you working?
N: Yeah. I'm a researcher – attached to the university there. I'm doing work on climate change.
G: Wow, interesting. And are you presenting at the conference?
N: Yeah. I was on yesterday, actually. What about you?
G: No, goodness! The whole idea really scares me. I don't think I could do it. I'm happy just attending and going to the talks.

▶ TRACKS 2 & 3

1 Do you know it?
2 Did you enjoy it?
3 Have you studied here before?
4 Where are you based?
5 What are you doing there? Are you working?
6 How long have you been learning French?

▶ TRACK 4

1

A: What are you studying?
B: Media studies.
A: Oh right. What does that involve? I've never heard of that subject.
B: Really? It's quite popular here. You study everything about TV, newspapers and advertising. Some of it's practical and some of it is more theoretical, almost like philosophy. It's really interesting.

2

C: Have you studied here before?
D: No, never.
C: How long have you been studying English?
D: For about five years now, but only for two hours a week.

3

E: What do you do when you're not studying?
F: I love movies and reading and I'm really into music. I play the guitar in a band.
E: Oh really? What kind of music are you into?
F: Garage, punk and rock'n'roll.

4

G: Do you have any brothers or sisters?
H: Yeah, I've got one older sister.
G: Do you get on with her OK?
H: Yeah, really well. We're very close.

5

I: What did you do at the weekend?
J: Nothing much. I went shopping on Saturday, but that's all.
I: Oh right. Did you get anything nice?
J: Yeah, I did actually. I got this really nice jacket in the market.

6

K: What do you do?
L: I'm a computer programmer.
K: Oh yeah? Who do you work for?
L: A small educational technology company in the centre of town.

TRACK 5

1

I was in town and I was walking down the main street and two Chinese guys came up to me and stopped me. They showed me a business card and pointed at a map on their phone. They just said, 'Donde, donde? Where, where?' So I said in Chinese, 'I don't know.' They first looked really surprised and then they started talking really fast, you know, and I didn't catch anything at all! I asked them to slow down, and then, with a mixture of my bad Chinese and gesture, I explained they had put the wrong postcode in the phone and they needed to go to another part of the city. I was quite proud of myself. After three years of study, it was actually the first time I'd spoken to anyone Chinese outside of my class and it really motivated me. Since then I've found someone to practise with.

2

I'm Brazilian so I speak Portuguese, but I speak German at home. People are interested when they find out, but they're amazed when I say my parents are from Russia and Turkey! They say, 'Wow! How's that?' Well, they first met when they were both working on a cruise ship. He worked in the engine room and she was a cabin cleaner. The ship's crew had a kind of party each week and they met there. My mum said Dad was a really good dancer, which I find very difficult to believe. Anyway, neither spoke each other's language, but my mum had worked in Germany before and Dad knew German from school, so that's how they communicated. They chose to settle in Rio because the cruises usually stopped here and when they were married they often had a short holiday here. They also said it saved them arguing about whose country to live in.

3

I'm a sound engineer on a National Geographic show called *Beast Hunter*. We go all over the place in search of unusual wild animals and we often need the support of local people to act as guides or cooks for the film crew. I always try to learn a bit of their language to, you know, just connect somehow. Anyway, last year we were filming in Sumatra in the middle of a forest, looking for orangutans. And one time, at dinner, I was talking to the guide and I tried to ask about 'the people of the inner forest', but apparently I asked about 'people with tasty insides'. I thought the guide looked a bit worried and then later I found out that the presenter of the programme had previously tried to thank him for the meal and instead of saying the food's really delicious, had said 'I'm eating a child!' Who knows what they thought of us!

TRACKS 6 & 7

1 He was travelling around Europe by train.
2 people were getting off the train
3 when he was leaving the station
4 because he'd left his bag on the train
5 but it had gone
6 and was sitting there crying
7 what had happened
8 he was still living with his family, you see

UNIT 2

TRACK 8

1

R = Ryan, C = Clara

R: Hey, Clara!
C: What is it, Ryan?
R: Have you seen Karim this week?
C: Yeah, I saw him yesterday. Why?
R: Is he OK? I haven't spoken to him for a while, but the last time I saw him he seemed a bit down.
C: Hmm, I know. I think it's his mum. Apparently, she's quite ill and he's just very worried about her.
R: Oh no! That sounds like a nightmare. What's wrong with her? Is it very serious?
C: I think it must be. He was quite upset when I spoke to him and he didn't want to say much.
R: Oh dear. That's awful. I feel a bit guilty now that I haven't rung him – I had a feeling something was wrong.
C: Why?
R: Well, I met him outside the university with Chris. Chris and I were chatting, but Karim didn't say much. In fact, he hardly said anything at all.
C: Really?
R: And Karim is normally really chatty.
C: I know. Well, he probably isn't in the mood to talk to anyone at the moment.
R: Oh dear. Well, if you see him, tell him I'm thinking of him. Say 'hello' to him from me.
C: Sure.

2

B = Belinda, A = Alisha

B: Hello Alisha! How's it going?
A: Great actually, Belinda. I've just finished all my exams!
B: That must be a relief. How did they go?
A: Quite well, I think. I was really pleased with how I did.
B: That's great.
A: Are you all right? You look as if you need cheering up.
B: Yeah, sorry. I'm just a bit fed up with the situation with my accommodation.
A: Oh dear. What's the problem?
B: Oh, I've just found out I can't continue to stay where I am at the moment.
A: What a pain! How come?
B: Basically, I need to find something else and, to be honest, I just don't need the stress.
A: I can imagine. Can I do anything to help?
B: No, it's OK. I'm sure it'll sort itself out, but thanks.
A: Well, at least let me buy you a drink.
B: OK. That'd be nice.
A: What would you like?
B: A cappuccino would be good.
A: Anything else? A bit of cake? Go on. It'll cheer you up.
B: Well, I have to say that chocolate cake looks nice.
A: I think I'll join you – to celebrate finishing my exams.

Audio scripts 105

▶ TRACK 9

1
A: I can't drink at the moment. I'm pregnant.
B: Really? Congratulations! When's the baby due?

2
A: I'm going to Canada to study English.
B: Wow! That's great! How long are you going for?

3
A: I'm afraid I can't meet you tonight.
B: Oh, what a shame! Are you sure?

4
A: My brother's not very well.
B: Oh no! I'm really sorry. I hope it's not too serious.

5
A: I've lost my wallet.
B: Oh no! What a pain! Did it have much in it?

6
A: I've found my wallet!
B: Phew, that's a relief! Where was it?

▶ TRACK 10

Having seen his Free Hugs campaign attract the attention of the world's media, Juan Mann wrote a book called *The Illustrated Guide to Free Hugs*, became a well-known public speaker and published his mobile number online, offering to go out for dinner with anyone who contacted him. In the meantime, however, his then-friend Shimon Moore, who had initially posted the video on YouTube, found his band was getting offered record deals. They moved to Los Angeles and started selling Free Hugs goods at concerts. And that's where it all went wrong.

By 2010, the pair had fallen out, with Mann claiming that he hadn't earned any money at all from the sales. He now leads a quiet life well away from the public eye, while Moore is still promoting the Free Hugs 'brand', and what a brand it's become: there's now an annual international Free Hugs Day; Free Hugs have been used to raise awareness of HIV and AIDS in some countries, while in others the movement is viewed with suspicion and huggers have been arrested.

Even though its founder is no longer actively involved, it seems that, in the end, free hugs are about more than Juan Mann!

▶ TRACK 11

R = Robin, C = Carla

R: Carla! Hey! Fancy seeing you here.
C: Um ... sorry, but do I know you?
R: It's me, Robin. From school?
C: Robin! Wow! WOW! Sorry. I just didn't recognise you. You look so ... different.
R: Oh, um, yeah. I guess. Anyway, how are you? You're looking really well.
C: Thanks. I'm fine, yeah. I'm good.
R: What are you doing here?
C: Oh, I work quite near here. I'm just on my lunch break, actually.
R: Oh really? Where do you work?
C: Just round the corner actually. I do sales and marketing for a film company.
R: That's amazing. I'm really pleased for you. You sound like you're doing really well.
C: Thanks. I'm enjoying it. It's hard work, though. I mean, we're setting up a new website at the moment, so I'm working really long hours. I'm not finishing till nine most days.
R: Really? You must be exhausted.
C: Yeah. But it's fun and I'm learning a lot and the money's not bad either, so I can't complain.
R: And are you still with your boyfriend? What was his name?
C: Cass? Yeah, we're engaged now, actually. We're getting married in the summer.
R: Really? Wow! Congratulations! That's great.
C: Thanks. Anyway, enough about me. How are you? What are you doing these days?
R: Me? Oh, you know ... nothing much, actually. I mean, I'm not really working or anything. I'm just kind of taking my time, thinking about what I want to do, you know.
C: OK. And are you still living at home?
R: Yeah. Yeah, I am. I can't really afford a place of my own at the moment.
C: Right. How's your mum? Is she OK?
R: She's fine, yeah. She's away at the moment, actually. She's staying with her brother on the coast.
C: Oh, nice.
R: She remembers you, you know. She still talks about you from time to time.
C: That's nice to know. Say 'hello' to her from me.
R: I will, yeah. Anyway, it's good to see you again.
C: Yeah, you too. We must meet again sometime.
R: Yeah, let's. Listen, what are you doing this Saturday? Do you want to meet for lunch or something?
C: Oh, I'd love to, but I train on Saturdays. I'm doing the marathon next month.
R: Rather you than me!
C: Oh, I love running – I'm really looking forward to it.
R: I have to say, that's my idea of hell! But still, good luck with it.
C: Thanks.

▶ TRACK 12

1 How's your course going?
2 I'm finding it a lot harder than before.
3 Is she still studying?
4 She's doing a Master's.
5 Is it still raining outside?
6 It's pouring down.
7 I'm meeting an old friend of mine for dinner.
8 Why's he shouting at everyone like that?

REVIEW 1

▶ TRACK 13

1 You look as if you need to go to bed.
2 What are you doing after the class? Do you fancy a coffee?
3 We're going out for dinner later. Do you want to join us?
4 We met when we were working at the same law firm.
5 Sorry, what did you say? I didn't hear.
6 I'd forgotten to put it in my diary.

UNIT 3

▶ TRACK 14

1 it's about ten miles out of town
2 you can walk along the walls
3 it's in the financial district
4 it's down by the beach
5 it's further along the coast
6 you find them all over this area

TRACK 15

C = Claire, R = Receptionist
C: Hello there. I wonder if you can help me. I'm thinking of going sightseeing today. Can you recommend anywhere good to go?
R: Well, it depends on what you like. There are lots of places to choose from. What kinds of things are you interested in?
C: I don't know. Um, something cultural?
R: Oh, right. OK. Well, quite close to here is St Mary's Church. It's Kraków's most famous church – and very beautifully decorated. You can walk there in five or ten minutes.
C: OK. I'm not really a big fan of churches, to be honest.
R: That's OK, I understand. Of course, the most visited place near here is Auschwitz. There's a day tour leaving soon.
C: Actually, we're planning on going there later in the week.
R: Well, in that case, you could try Kazimierz, the old Jewish Quarter, where Steven Spielberg filmed some of *Schindler's List*. It's actually quite a lively area now. There are lots of good bars and restaurants round there.
C: Oh, so that might be nice for this evening, then.
R: Yes, maybe. Let me know if you want more information about places to eat or drink there. Erm, then if you'd prefer something a bit different, how about a guided tour of Nowa Huta, the old communist district? They'll show you what life was like in the old days there.
C: Oh, that sounds interesting. How much is that?
R: About €40. I can call and book a place for you if you want.
C: What times does that leave?
R: Every two hours from outside the hotel and the tours last around 90 minutes. They leave at 10 o'clock, 12 o'clock, 2 o'clock and 4 o'clock.
C: OK, that's great. Can you book me onto the 2 o'clock tour? Then I can do some shopping in the main square in town beforehand.
R: Sure.

TRACK 16

1
A: I'm thinking of doing some shopping today. Can you recommend anywhere?
B: Well, you could try Oxford Street. There are lots of big department stores there.
A: To be honest, I'm not really a big fan of department stores.
B: Oh, OK. Well, in that case, how about Portobello Road? It's a big street market. You can find lots of bargains there.
A: Oh, that sounds great. I love that kind of thing. Is it easy to get to?
B: Yes, very. I'll show you on the map.

2
C: I'm thinking of doing some sightseeing today. Can you recommend anywhere?
D: Well, you could try the local museum. That's quite close to here. They've got lots of interesting things in there.
C: Right. I'm not really into museums, to be honest.
D: That's OK. In that case, how about going to the Roman ruins down by the lake? There are also some nice cafés and you can swim there.
C: Oh, that sounds better. Are they expensive to get into?
D: No, it's quite cheap. It should only be about $10.

TRACK 17

1
In July and August it's boiling hot here. The temperature regularly rises to above 40 degrees and sometimes even reaches 50, so we often try to get away. We went to Malaysia last year. This year we're going to Salalah. The weather is wonderful then – light rain most days, cloud from the sea and cool, it's never much more than 25 degrees. At night we can even say it's chilly. Wonderful. Such a relief to escape the heat. We're staying in a five-star hotel, of course. This is important for my family because my mother and sisters spend a lot of time in and around the hotel. But my father and I, we love driving off-road – four by four. At home we drive in the desert, but the countryside in south Oman is mountainous and so green. It offers something different. So we'll probably hire a car to do off-road.

2
The summer's a busy time of year. I work from May through to September and this year I have to work long hours in July and August. When the season ends, I might take a short holiday, but if I do, I'll probably just go and visit a friend in Lyon. Basically, I'm saving money because I'm going to travel round Vietnam later in the year. I've heard it's best to visit after October because it's still warm but not so humid. Not that the weather is so important. What's important to me is the experience of travel. I went to Morocco last year and I was in the desert near these ancient ruins. I was in a small hostel and it was freezing at night, but the people and place, the experience – it was fantastic.

3
We've decided we're not going to go on holiday this year. We're just going to stay at home. Last year's holiday was such a nightmare. We rented a small cottage near the beach in Cornwall, but it poured with rain most of the time and the kids complained so much. 'Ooh, there's nothing to do.' 'Aargh! My phone's got no signal!' Constant. And it wasn't cheap. So, this year, instead of spending the money on travel and accommodation, we're going to spend it on doing nice things here. So, we're thinking of going to a show or two, we might visit Buckingham Palace and the British Museum, which, believe it or not, I've never been to! Maybe a boat trip down the river, and also just relax at home in the garden for a change as well. And the kids want to go paintballing with some friends. And then there are all the great restaurants here. We're going to eat out every night. I don't know why we haven't done it before.

UNIT 4

TRACK 18

1

A = Alan, B = Brenda
A: So what did you do last night Brenda? Anything interesting?
B: Yeah, I went to the theatre, actually, and saw this amazing play.
A: Oh really? Which one?
B: It's called *Routes*. Have you seen it?
A: I don't think so. What was it like?
B: Oh, it was great. A bit depressing, but really interesting. I enjoyed it.
A: So, do you go to the theatre a lot, then?
B: Yeah, quite a lot, I guess. Maybe two or three times a month.
A: Wow! That's impressive. I hardly ever go. I can't even remember the last time I went!

Audio scripts 107

2

C = Charlotte, D = Domi

C: Did you have a good weekend Domi?
D: Yeah, it was great. I went sailing with some friends. We went along the coast as far as Guernsey and then came back. And it was boiling as well, so I got a bit of a suntan.
C: Wow! I didn't know you sailed. How often do you do that?
D: Not as much as I used to, to be honest. When I was living in Brittany, I went all the time, but I don't often get the chance now. That's kind of what made it really special, you know.
C: Yeah.
D: Have you ever been?
C: No, never, but I'd love to. It looks amazing.
D: Well, next time we go, I'll let you know.

3

E = Evan, F = Frank

E: Are you OK, Frank? You look a bit tired.
F: I know. I didn't go to bed until two thirty.
E: Really? Why?
F: Oh, some friends of mine came over and we sat up late playing cards and talking and stuff.
E: Oh really? I play cards sometimes too. Are you any good?
F: Yeah, I'm OK. I mean, I'm not a professional or anything, but I enjoy it.
E: Do you ever play poker?
F: Yeah, quite often, actually. It's my dad's favourite game, so we play together when we meet.
E: OK. That's nice. Well, maybe we could play together sometime.

▶ TRACK 19

1

A: So do you go the theatre a lot, then?
B: Yeah, quite a lot, I guess. Maybe two or three times a month.

2

C: I didn't know you sailed. How often do you do that?
D: Not as much as I used to, to be honest. When I was living in Brittany, I went all the time, but I don't often get the chance now.

3

E: Do you ever play poker?
F: Yeah, quite often, actually.

▶ TRACK 20

1 Do you go swimming a lot?
2 Do you eat out a lot?
3 So do you read much?
4 Do you go to the cinema much?
5 How often do you play games on the computer?
6 So how often do you go to the gym?
7 Do you ever try to read in English?
8 Do you ever watch your favourite team play?

▶ TRACK 21

I = Ian, R = Rika

I: What happened there, Rika? Did you just sign that guy's book?
R: You saw that?
I: Yeah! It was like you were famous or something.
R: That's because, er … I don't know. I guess I am, kind of – if you're a judo fan.
I: What?
R: Well, in my other life, away from selling books, I do judo and last week I was in a competition on TV. That guy recognised me from there.
I: Seriously? That's amazing!
R: Oh, it's no big deal. I didn't win it or anything. I lost in the semi-finals.
I: You got to the semi-finals! I can't believe it! I mean, no offence, but you don't look big enough to fight.
R: Well, you fight according to your weight in judo, so size doesn't matter. Although being big isn't always an advantage. It's more about balance. Someone can be big and strong, but if they're off-balance, you can easily throw them. I bet I could throw you over!
I: Hey, I believe you! So how long have you been doing it, then?
R: Ever since I was a kid. At school, the big kids often used to bully me because I was so small and I got into fights, so my dad suggested I did a martial art to defend myself and that was it, really.
I: Well, you've kept very quiet about it. I mean, how long have I known you now? Six years?
R: Yeah, well, I don't really feel like it's connected to what I do at work and, I don't know, I think it's strange for me to just tell colleagues I'm a judo champion for no reason.
I: I guess. So, how often do you have to train?
R: Well, I usually practise all the techniques for at least an hour a day once I get home in the evening, and then two or three times a week I go to a special judo school to practise fighting.
I: Wow! And this competition the other week … what was it exactly? Was it a big thing?
R: Um, yeah … it was the women's national finals!
I: No! And you got to the semi-finals!
R: Yeah! I've actually won it before so I'm a bit annoyed I didn't win it this time, but I had quite a bad back injury last year, which stopped me doing any training or fighting.
I: Really? How long were you out of action?
R: Well, I didn't do anything for a couple of months and I only started full training a few weeks before the finals.
I: OK. Well, it sounds as if you did well to get to the semi-finals then.
R: I guess. And the girl who beat me went on to win the whole thing, so … still, I hate losing!
I: Amazing. You learn something new every day!

▶ TRACK 22

1 How long has he been driving?
2 How long have you been doing that?
3 How long did you play for?
4 How long was he injured?
5 How long did you warm up for?
6 How long have they been married?
7 How long has she been learning?
8 How long have you been waiting?

▶ TRACK 23

A: Do you listen to music much?
B: Yeah, all the time.
A: What kind of music are you into?
B: All sorts, really, but mainly pop music and R&B.
A: Oh right. Anyone in particular?
B: Erm, I don't know … Girls Rock, Soul Train, stuff like that.
A: So, have you heard anything good recently?
B: Well, I downloaded this great song by K Boy. It's fantastic.

REVIEW 2

▶ TRACK 24
1 How long have you been doing that?
2 I'll probably just stay in and have an early night.
3 I might go to a friend's house and play cards.
4 Not as much as I should, to be honest.
5 How long has he been injured?
6 No never, but I'd love to.

UNIT 5

▶ TRACK 25

I = Ivan, A = Amanda

I: So what do you do, Amanda?
A: I work for a mobile phone company.
I: Oh yeah? Doing what?
A: I work in the design department. I'm involved in designing what you see on the screen of the phone. You know, all the graphics and icons.
I: Oh right. Sounds interesting. How did you get into that?
A: Well, I studied graphic design. After I graduated, I worked for a company that designed websites. Then one day I saw Vodafone were recruiting people so I applied and I got a job. They gave me some training and I just got into it that way.
I: OK. So how long have you been working there?
A: It must be seven years now. Wait! No, eight! I was 25 when I joined, so yeah, eight years. Time goes so fast!
I: You must enjoy it.
A: Yeah, I do generally. It's quite varied because they're constantly changing the phones and designs, and of course it's quite a creative job, which is nice. But, you know, it's like any job. It has its boring moments and the hours can be quite long.
I: Really? How long?
A: Well, it depends if we have a deadline to meet, but sometimes I do something like fifty or sixty hours a week.
I: Really? That can't be easy.
A: It's actually fine. I mean, it is a bit stressful sometimes, but you get used to it. In fact, I sometimes need that stress to work well, you know. I sometimes work better under pressure.
I: Really? I can't work like that.
A: So what do you do?
I: Oh, nothing! At the moment, I'm just studying.
A: Really? How old did you say you are?
I: Thirty.
A: Really? You look younger.
I: Thanks.
A: So were you working before?
I: Kind of. I worked in a law firm two years ago, but it was really insecure. When I started, I was basically working for free, more or less. I mean, they covered my lunch and my travel costs, but basically I didn't get paid.
A: Seriously?
I: Yeah. And, of course, I didn't mind to begin with. I needed the work experience and they were a well-respected firm. I guess I just expected that sooner or later they'd offer me a full-time job.
A: And did they?
I: No, not a chance! There were some vague promises – enough to keep me thinking I might get something – but in the end I realised it was never going to happen.
A: How long were you there?
I: Just over a year and a half!
A: That's terrible.
I: Yeah, but you know, it happens quite a lot. Anyway, now I'm preparing for government exams, so I can get a civil service job. It's much more secure. It's almost a job for life.
A: Really? That must be very competitive if other jobs are so insecure and badly paid.
I: Yeah, it is. I think there were a thousand people applying for ten jobs last time.
A: Gosh. Well, good luck.

▶ TRACK 26
1 That must be quite demanding.
2 That must be great.
3 You can't find that very easy.
4 She must earn a fortune.
5 That must be really rewarding.
6 That can't be much fun.
7 That must be a worry.
8 You must be doing well.

▶ TRACK 27

A

D = Dom, L = Laura

D: Did you hear about Patrick?
L: No. What?
D: Apparently, he's been given a written warning.
L: You're joking! What for?
D: He was going on the Internet to buy concert tickets and book holidays. And he was always sending personal emails.
L: Yeah? So what? Doesn't everyone do that? I mean, we're certainly allowed to do it in our breaks.
D: Well, apparently, you're not allowed to use the company computers like that at all. Not in his company, anyway.
L: That's a bit unfair, isn't it?
D: You say that, but actually what happened to him was he visited some site or other and somehow got a computer virus and then it infected the whole system. He said the company had to spend a fortune sorting it all out.
L: Oh right. Well, in that case, I can see why they might be a bit angry, then!

B

F = Francesca, J = Jade

F: Are you thinking of buying that?
J: Yeah, what do you think?
F: Very smart. I don't usually see you wearing stuff like that.
J: No, I know, but I've got this new job working in a law firm.
F: Oh really? That's great news! What are you going to be doing there?
J: Just admin work really, but they have a strict dress code – you can't even wear smart trousers; you have to wear skirts!
F: You're joking! Is that legal?
J: I guess so. They can do what they want, can't they?
F: You think? What if you can't wear something for religious or health reasons?
J: I don't know! I guess they make an exception. Anyway, listen, I've been looking for a job for ages so I'm not going to complain!

C

A = Adam, B = Bill

A: Bill, sorry to interrupt, but can I have a quick word?
B: Yes, of course. What's up?
A: Listen, I'd like to take the day off on Friday. My son's performing in a school concert.
B: Friday? I'm afraid that's impossible.
A: Are you sure?
B: Sorry, Adam. It wouldn't be a problem normally, but we've got a bit of a crisis this week. Vicky's off sick and we really have to complete this order by Saturday.
A: Can't someone else help? My son will be so disappointed if I don't watch him play. And I do have some holiday left for this year.
B: I'm sure. But if we're late with this order, we might lose the whole contract.
A: I see.
B: You're supposed to arrange time off with me a month in advance, you know.
A: I know, I know. It's just I've asked you at short notice before and it hasn't been a problem.
B: Well, as I say, normally it isn't.
A: Well, I guess that's all. I don't know what I'll tell my son.
B: I'm sorry. You'll be really helping me and the company.

▶ TRACK 28

to it
get used to it
have to get used to it
I'll have to get used to it
I guess I'll have to get used to it.

UNIT 6

▶ TRACK 29

S = Sales assistant, C = Customer

S: Hello there. Can I help you?
C: Yeah, hi. I'm thinking of changing phone companies.
S: Alright. Well, you've come to the right place! Who are you with at the moment?
C: Blue. But I'm looking to see if there are any better deals around.
S: I'm sure we can find you something. What phone do you have at the moment?
C: This one, but they've offered to upgrade it to the S620.
S: OK, that's a nice phone. And what are the monthly payments on that?
C: £30 a month.
S: OK. Well, I think we could offer you something better. For example, this one – the N570.
C: OK. What's the difference? They look pretty similar to me.
S: Well, with this one, the N570, you get a much better user experience. It's a bit easier to navigate and, as you can see, the screen folds out so it's about twice the size of your current phone's.
C: Wow! That is nice.
S: I know. It's impressive, isn't it? It's got a great battery life as well. It uses a lithium-ion battery, while the other phone uses a polymer battery, which isn't as good. It usually needs recharging after ten hours, whereas the lithium-ion one lasts up to twelve hours longer.
C: Oh, OK.
S: And then the camera is much more powerful. So this one is 32 megapixels and has an excellent digital zoom, whereas the one on the S620 is just fifteen.
C: Right. And how many pictures can the N570 store?
S: It holds up to 6,000 – that's three times the capacity of the S620 – though obviously it depends on what else you're storing on there. And, of course, you can always just store all your images in the Cloud if you'd prefer.
C: OK. And what about sound quality?
S: Well, the N570 has a fairly large speaker built in on the back here. See? It's about twice as big as the speaker you currently have, so no worries there.
C: OK. Well, I must admit, it is a nice phone. I'm tempted. What about calls and text messages? How many can you offer me?
S: Well, for £45 a month we could give you 700 free minutes and 400 texts.
C: 400! That's quite a lot less than Blue are offering me.
S: Well, I'm not sure we can give much more for that phone. What do you get with them?
C: 800 free minutes and 600 texts.
S: OK. Well, we could probably match that and still give you the better phone.

▶ TRACK 30

1
I don't like souvenirs like magnets or key rings. They're a waste of money. Better to have something you can consume. My neighbour's Italian and he gave us this delicious fruit cake. Apparently, it's very typical. Oh, what do you call it … um … comes in a box … oh, *Panettone* – that's it! Anyway, yeah, I also went to Malta recently and we bought a bottle of drink made from prickly pears. Lovely. We finished the drink in about two days, but I kept the bottle as it was actually perfect for keeping oil in.

2
My wife's an English teacher and she gets all kinds of presents from her students – and I know I'm going to sound ungrateful – but I don't want them! One student gave her a present for me. It was a horrible bright silk tie with a picture of the Great Wall of China printed on it! Another time we had this plastic model of the Eiffel Tower with a light in it. I mean, I'm a designer! Why do I need these things? My wife refuses to throw them away, though, so we keep them in a box under the stairs and I agree to display one item each month in the kitchen.

3
One of my friends spent last summer travelling round Europe by train and she brought me back an apron from Lithuania, I think it was, to wear while I'm cooking. It's the best souvenir I've ever had. It's made from this beautiful hand-woven material and it has a lovely stripy pattern which she said is typical from there. She's clever, because she knows I love cooking and she's also seen the mess I make when I cook. Maybe I'll look less scruffy now!

4
I visited Greece last year and we went to Athens. As a souvenir, my daughter bought a glass paperweight with an image of the Parthenon inside. She was really happy with it. Then on the way home, the airline lost our luggage. The paperweight was in her bag so she was upset, but then they found the bags and when they arrived the paperweight was there and it was fine. Big relief! But then, she was putting it on her shelf and she dropped it! Oh dear, she was so upset! She cried for ages.

TRACK 31

S = Seller, B = Buyer

S: Yes darlin'. You like the jacket?
B: Yeah, it's nice. How much is it?
S: Two hundred and fifty.
B: Two hundred and fifty! That's very expensive.
S: Not really. It's top quality. Feel it.
B: Hmm.
S: That's genuine leather. It'll last forever, that will.
B: Sure. It's nice. But two fifty?
S: How much do you wanna pay?
B: Well, I was thinking fifty.
S: Fifty! Come on!
B: OK, one hundred?
S: One hundred. You're insulting me! I won't make any money like that. Listen, I'll give it to you for two hundred.
B: Come on. I've seen similar ones that are cheaper. One fifty.
S: Similar, but not as good. Go on then! Go and buy it. You're wasting my time … OK, I tell you what, I'll do it for a hundred and ninety.
B: One sixty. I don't have much money left.
S: One hundred and eighty. Final offer. Take it or leave it. I can't go lower than that. Look, it's perfect on you. You look gorgeous.
B: It is nice … OK, one eighty.
S: Love, you drive a hard bargain. My wife'll kill me if she finds out how much I gave that away for! That's her summer holiday she's losing on that deal. You want anything else? Hand-printed T-shirts? Unique, they are. Look.

TRACK 32

1 Two hundred and fifty.
2 Two hundred and fifty!
3 One hundred.
4 One hundred!
5 One eighty.
6 One hundred and eighty!

REVIEW 3

TRACK 33

1 It must have been very difficult getting a job in the media.
2 It can't be easy getting by on such a low salary.
3 Working there is not as bad as you might think.
4 I don't think I'll ever get used to it, to be honest.
5 We're allowed to work from home one day a week.
6 This one has slightly better sound quality.

UNIT 7

TRACK 34

D = Daniel, P = Paulina

P: Wow. It's busy today.
D: I know, it's crazy. I was supposed to take a break an hour ago.
P: Yeah, I'm going back after I've had this coffee.
D: OK. Are you going to the thing for Holly's birthday later?
P: No, I can't. I have a class.
D: Oh yeah? What are you studying?
P: It's a counselling course for speech therapists.
D: Oh, right. What does that involve?
P: Well, you learn basic counselling skills. You know, how to listen and guide people through problems, but it's focused on the kinds of psychological problems people have when they have a difficulty with speaking.
D: And how come you're doing that?
P: Well, I did speech therapy at college and, you know, that's still what I want to do.
D: Oh right.
P: So it'll be good for my CV.
D: Yeah. I'm sure. So, how's it going? Are you enjoying it?
P: Yeah, it's good. It's very practical. I mean, we have some lectures and seminars which are about theory, but most of the time we just practise with each other and a tutor observes us and gives feedback.
D: So, what about the tutors? What are they like?
P: Great. They're all very experienced and knowledgeable, but they present things in a very clear way, you know, they're like on our level. They're really good, actually.
D: It sounds it. And what are the other students like? Do you get on with them OK?
P: Yeah, mostly.
D: Mostly?
P: Well, there are one or two guys that aren't as supportive as everyone else. Like when we do the feedback after the practice sessions, they can be a bit more critical than the others, which is a bit annoying.
D: I can imagine. You want encouragement, not criticism!
P: Exactly.
D: So how long does the course last? When do you finish?
P: I think there are eleven weeks left. It's a six-month course – an evening a week.
D: Do you have any coursework on top of that? I mean, is it assessed?
P: Not exactly. You just get a certificate for completing the course.
D: And to get that?
P: You have to attend 80% of the classes and do an assignment, which is basically a kind of diary of our counselling sessions – nothing too demanding.
D: OK. So you don't have to do much reading?
P: There's a bit connected to the seminars and you could do more, but I don't have time on top of my workload here.
D: I bet. So what are you going to do when it ends?
P: Well, I might actually do another course once I've finished this one.
D: Wow! You're keen!
P: Maybe, but as soon as I find a proper job, I'll probably stop doing any studying.
D: Sure.
P: I'd better get back.
D: OK.

TRACK 35

1
A: How's the class?
B: Awful! They just don't pay attention. If I try to explain something, they sit whispering to each other. It's so rude! And then there's one boy who always walks in twenty minutes late. He doesn't apologise. He just puts his mobile on the table, takes off his iPod and his Armani sunglasses, and then he sits there looking bored because he thinks he knows it all. He's got no pen, no paper, nothing. It's really annoying!
A: I think you need to set some rules. If they talk, send them to the headteacher or give them a detention.
B: Maybe. I don't want to be too strict.
A: But you have to be! If you're strict from the start, you'll gain their respect. Obviously, you need to be fair as well.

2

C: Are you OK? You look a bit fed up.
D: I've just got the results of my English test.
C: Oh dear. What did you get?
D: A 6. And I needed a 6.5 to do a Master's.
C: Oh no! I'm sorry. But you worked so hard. I was sure you'd get at least a 7.
D: I know. I was so stupid. I misread one of the questions. That probably lowered my score.
C: Oh dear. So, what are you going to do now?
D: It depends. I'm going to ring the course leader and see if they'll accept me with a 6. If they don't accept me on the course, I'll either retake the test or I might look for another Master's.

3

E: Right, there are a number of things I need to tell you about assessment. Firstly, 50% of your final marks are based on your essays during the course. Because of that, we're very strict on deadlines. If you miss a deadline that your tutor has set, you will be given a zero. No arguments! Secondly, er … yes?
F: Yeah, sorry to interrupt, but what if you have a family crisis, or something?
E: Well, obviously we'll make an exception for certain cases if a close family member is affected. Also, we won't accept any excuses to do with illness unless you produce a doctor's certificate within two days of the deadline. Does that answer your question? Good. I should say, while we're on the subject, that if you have any problems which are affecting your coursework, you should contact the student counselling service. Their number is …

4

G: So how's Angela doing at her new school?
H: Oh, much better, thanks. I'm so glad we decided to move her to St James's. The teachers seem a lot better prepared. And they push the kids. I think Angela was just a bit bored at her last school.
G: Well, she's a bright kid.
H: And that other school was quite rough. I was always hearing about fights in the playground and lots of kids there skip classes on a fairly regular basis as well.
G: Well, St James's has a very good reputation.
H: Yes. Discipline is very good there. And I think they look so much smarter in a uniform.
G: Hmm.

▶ TRACK 36

1 know – knowledge
2 analyse – analysis
3 assess – assessment
4 define – definition
5 inform – information
6 interpret – interpretation
7 worry – worry
8 increase – increase
9 refund – refund
10 protest – protest

UNIT 8

▶ TRACK 37

A = Aurora, C = Claes

A: They don't have an English menu, I'm afraid, Claes – just a Spanish one.
C: That's OK. You'll just have to talk me through it.
A: No problem. Well, for starters they've got Papa Rellena. That's balls of mashed potato, stuffed with beef, raisins and olives, and then deep-fried.
C: OK. That sounds very filling for a starter!
A: It can be, yeah. Then there's Anticuchos. That's a bit like a Peruvian kebab. It's sliced cow heart, very tender and juicy, grilled on a stick.
C: Right. To be honest, Aurora, I don't really like the idea of eating heart. I don't know why. I just don't.
A: That's OK. No problem. There are plenty of other dishes to choose from.
C: Sorry. Anyway, what's next? What's Ceviche?
A: Ceviche! That's Peru's national dish. Have you never tried it?
C: No, never.
A: Oh, you really should. It's delicious. It's basically raw fish marinated in lime juice or lemon juice and served with the local kind of potato and corn. You get lots of different kinds of Ceviche, using different fish and seafood.
C: OK. Well, I'll go for that, the Ceviche. What are you going to have?
A: The Tallarín Con Mariscos. It's a kind of spaghetti served with shrimps and prawns and squid.
C: Sounds great. And what about the main courses?
A: Well, the Bistec Apanado. That's steak, sliced very thinly and then fried and served with rice.
C: OK.
A: And then there are two rice dishes – Arroz Con Mariscos, which is rice with fresh seafood. It's a bit like a Spanish paella, but spicier. Then there's Arroz Con Pato, which is rice with duck. The Lomo Saltado is a kind of steak dish.
C: Another one? I don't really eat steak very much, to be honest. I tend to find it quite bland.
A: Bland? Not this one. It's cooked with tomatoes and onions and spices and things. It's really good. Honestly!
C: I'll take your word for it, but I don't really feel like steak tonight anyway.
A: OK. Well, finally, there's Seco De Cabrito. It's a kind of stew with goat meat in, young goat meat – and they serve it with beans on the side.
C: That sounds very tasty. And quite unusual too. I'll have that.

▶ TRACK 38

1

A: You know that restaurant in the main street?
B: What? The one that's always deserted?
A: That's it, yeah. Well, guess what?
B: What?
A: I walked past there this morning and there were loads of police everywhere outside, guys with guns – everything.
B: Seriously? How come?
A: I'm not sure, but I was wondering if it might be a front for something. You know, some gang using it to wash their dirty money – maybe what they've made from selling drugs or something.
B: Hmm, it wouldn't surprise me if it was. I don't think I've ever seen a single person eating there.

2

C: How's your fish?
D: Oh, it's OK, but I guess it might be better if it didn't have so much sauce on it.
C: There is a lot of it.
D: Yeah, and it's really overpowering. I mean, the sauce is quite rich so it really overpowers the taste of everything else.
C: Oh dear. Do you want to try some of mine?
D: Go on then. Here, try some of this as well. It's not that bad. Mmm … that's gorgeous! That steak is so tender! You don't want to swap, do you?
C: Erm, no thanks. I think I'll stick with my one. You can have another bite, though.

3

E: You won't believe what happened to me last night!
F: Go on. What?
E: Well, Jacques took me out to that new organic place up on the hill. You know the one I mean?
F: Erm, no. I guess I missed that.
E: Oh, it's called Green Revolution. It's been in the papers quite a bit. It's got very trendy décor and they only serve locally-sourced organic food, so it's all super healthy.
F: OK. It sounds very fancy.
E: It is! And it isn't cheap either. I mean, you wouldn't go there if you were paying yourself.
F: Right.
E: It is lovely, though. It looks out over the valley, you know.
F: Nice.
E: Yeah, but the crazy thing was, we arrived and sat down and asked for the menu and literally that second, I saw this rat go running into the kitchen!
F: Ugh! Seriously? So, what did you do? Did you leave?
E: I wanted to, yeah, but Jacques just joked and said it must be an organic rat so it'd be fine.
F: Really? I'd be out of the door in an instant if that happened to me.

4

G: When did we ask for the bill?
H: I don't know. At least half an hour ago!
G: I know they're busy, but this is ridiculous. I think we should just go …
H: What? Without paying? Are you mad?
G: Well, they don't seem to want our money, do they?
H: Don't be ridiculous. I mean, what would happen if they called the police?
G: They wouldn't do that. Anyway, the restaurant doesn't deserve the money. I mean, the food wasn't that great.
H: The asparagus was OK.
G: Yeah, but the portions weren't very generous, were they? That lamb was much too spicy and then everything else was just a bit bland.
H: Yes, but you can't just leave without paying, can you?
G: No, I suppose not!

▶ TRACK 39

1 I'd complain if that happened to me.
2 I'd go crazy if I worked in a kitchen.
3 I'd be in trouble if I had to cook for myself every day.
4 If they tried to charge me for water, I'd just refuse to pay.
5 I'd come with you if I wasn't working tomorrow.
6 I wouldn't eat that even if you paid me!

REVIEW 4

▶ TRACK 40

1 I would if I could, but I can't.
2 I'll do it once I've done this.
3 I tend not to, no.
4 I think I'd find that off-putting.
5 What if they don't get back to us?
6 That sounds great. I'll go for that.

NATIONAL GEOGRAPHIC
LEARNING

Outcomes Intermediate
Student's Book Split A
Hugh Dellar and Andrew Walkley

Publisher: Gavin McLean
Publishing Consultant: Karen Spiller
Development Editor: Katy Wright
Editorial Manager: Claire Merchant
Head of Strategic Marketing ELT: Charlotte Ellis
Senior Content Project Manager: Nick Ventullo
Senior Production Controller: Eyvett Davis
Cover design: emc design
Text design: Alex Dull
Compositor: emc design
National Geographic Liaison:
  Wesley Della Volla / Leila Hishmeh
Audio: Tom Dick & Debbie Productions Ltd
DVD: Tom Dick & Debbie Productions Ltd

© 2016 National Geographic Learning, a Cengage Learning Company

ALL RIGHTS RESERVED. No part of this work covered by the copyright herein may be reproduced or distributed in any form or by any means, except as permitted by U.S. copyright law, without the prior written permission of the copyright owner.

"National Geographic", "National Geographic Society" and the Yellow Border Design are registered trademarks of the National Geographic Society ® Marcas Registradas

For product information and technology assistance, contact us at
Cengage Learning Customer & Sales Support, cengage.com/contact

For permission to use material from this text or product, submit all requests online at **cengage.com/permissions**
Further permissions questions can be emailed to
permissionrequest@cengage.com

Student's Book Split A ISBN: 978-1-337-56120-4

National Geographic Learning
Cheriton House, North Way, Andover, Hampshire, SP10 5BE
United Kingdom

National Geographic Learning, a Cengage Learning Company, has a mission to bring the world to the classroom and the classroom to life. With our English language programs, students learn about their world by experiencing it. Through our partnerships with National Geographic and TED Talks, they develop the language and skills they need to be successful global citizens and leaders.

Locate your local office at **international.cengage.com/region**

Visit National Geographic Learning online at **NGL.Cengage.com/ELT**
Visit our corporate website at **www.cengage.com**

CREDITS
Although every effort has been made to contact copyright holders before publication, this has not always been possible. If contacted, the publisher will undertake to rectify any errors or omissions at the earliest opportunity.

Printed in Greece by Bakis SA
Print Number: 02   Print Year: 2017

Photos

6–7 © Aaron Huey/National Geographic Creative; 8 © David Lees/Getty Images; 11 (t) © Mary Evans Picture Library; 11 (b) Mezzofanti's Gift published by Duckworth Overlook; 12 © Kseniya Ragozina/Getty Images; 13 © Ttstudio/Shutterstock.com; 14–15 © Joel Sartore/National Geographic Creative; 16 (l) © Cultura RM/Hugh Whitaker/Getty Images; 16 (m) © Jason Edwards/National Geographic Creative; 16 (r) © Scott Houston/Corbis; 17 (l) © ZANE GABRIEL MERCURIO/National Geographic Creative; 17 (m) © Alex Treadway/National Geographic Creative; 17 (r) © David Turnley/Corbis; 19 © Alex Hinds/Alamy; 20 © Michael Prince/Corbis; 21 © Blue Images/Corbis; 22 © Randy Olson/National Geographic Creative; 24–25 © Mike Theiss/National Geographic Creative; 27 © Zarnell/Getty Images; 28 (tl) © Corina Dragan/Getty Images; 28 (tr) © PhongTranVN/Getty Images; 28 (mtl) © Zubaida Yahya/Getty Images; 28 (mtr) © Ann Johansson/Corbis; 28 (mbl) © Tom Wang/Shutterstock.com; 28 (mbr) © arturasker/Shutterstock.com; 28 (bl) © eurobanks/Shutterstock.com; 28 (br) © dbimages/Alamy; 31 (tl) © Sergei Supinsky/Getty Images; 31 (tr) © balounm/Shutterstock.com; 31 (m) © Justin Black/Shutterstock.com; 31 (b) © Karen Kasmauski/National Geographic Creative; 32–33 © Karen Kasmauski/National Geographic Creative; 34–35 © Robin Moore/National Geographic Creative/Corbis; 36 (l) © xPACIFICA/National Geographic Creative; 36 (r) © Manca Juvan/In Pictures/Corbis; 37 (l) © PhotoStock10/Shutterstock.com; 37 (r) © imageBROKER/Alamy; 39 (tl) © John A. Angelillo/Corbis; 39 (tr) © Pictorial Press Ltd/Alamy; 39 (bl) © Alessandro Della Bella/epa/Corbis; 39 (br) © DENIS BALIBOUSE/Reuters/Corbis; 40 (t) © David Boyer/National Geographic Creative; 40 (b) © Georg Gerster/National Geographic Creative; 42–43 © Hoberman Collection/UIG via Getty Images; 44 © Paul Hardy/Corbis; 47 (t) © Richard Jolley/CartoonStock; 47 (m) © Dave Carpenter/CartoonStock; 47 (b) © Baloo (Rex May)/CartoonStock; 48 (t) © Imaginechina/Corbis; 48 (b) © Adam Wiseman/Corbis; 50–51 © Scott Stulberg/Corbis; 52 © andresr/Getty Images; 54 (l) © David Alan Harvey/National Geographic Creative; 54 (m) © James P. Blair/National Geographic Creative; 54 (r) © Stewart Cohen Pictures/Purestock/SuperStock/Corbis; 55 (l) © Charlie Nucci/Corbis; 55 (m) © Timur Emek/Getty Images; 55 (r) © Michael Nichols/National Geographic Creative; 56 (ml) © Quasarphoto/Getty Images; 56 (tr) © John Bradley/Getty Images; 56 (mr) © Leeman/Getty Images; 56 (tl) © Manakin/Getty Images; 56 (tm) © FernandoGM/Getty Images; 56 (mm) © sylwia kania/Getty Images; 56 (bl) © Sohadiszno/Getty Images; 56 (bm) © Jitchanamont/Shutterstock.com; 56 (br) © levers2007/Getty Images; 58 © Stuart Dee/Getty Images; 60–61 © Pete Ryan/National Geographic Creative; 62–63 © James L. Stanfield/National Geographic Creative; 64 © Dave Bartruff/Corbis; 67 © Kike Calvo/National Geographic Creative; 68–69 © Fritz Hoffmann/National Geographic Creative; 71 (t) © CarlaNichiata/Getty Images; 71 (b) © Christian Vinces/Shutterstock.com; 72 © xPACIFICA/Corbis; 73 © Martin Thomas Photography/Alamy; 74 © Atlantide Phototravel/Corbis; 76 © Brent Hofacker/Shutterstock.com; 78 © Blue Images/Corbis; 80–81 © OJO Images Ltd /Alamy; 82 © Hans Berggren/Johnér Images/Corbis; 84–85 © istocksdaily/Getty Images; 97 (tl) © Shikhar Bhattarai/Getty Images; 97 (tml) © Image Source Pink/Thinkstock; 97 (tmr) © NADOFOTOS/Getty Images; 97 (tr) © Ingram Publishing/Getty Images; 97 (bl) © Purestock/Getty Images; 97 (bml) © Wavebreakmedia Ltd/Getty Images; 97 (bmr) © Evgeny Sergeev/Getty Images; 97 (br) © Fuse/Getty Images; 101 (tl) © Laboko/Shutterstock.com; 101 (tml) © JIANG HONGYAN/Shutterstock.com; 101 (tmm) © amphaiwan/Shutterstock.com; 101 (tmr) © JIANG HONGYAN/Shutterstock.com; 101 (tr) © AlexRaths/Getty Images; 101 (ml) © Artville; 101 (mml) © Nikola Bilic/Shutterstock.com; 101 (mmm) © DeluXe-PiX/Getty Images; 101 (mmr) © Magone/Getty Images; 101 (mr) © PhotoDisc/Getty Images; 101 (bl) © graletta/Getty Images; 101 (bml) © bonchan/Shutterstock.com; 101 (bmr) © Crepesoles/Shutterstock.com; 101 (br) © PhotoDisc/Getty Images; 102 (t) © Andrey Bayda/Shutterstock.com; 102 (b) © Paul Prescott/Shutterstock.com.

Cover
Cover photograph © Mauricio Abreu/JAI/Corbis.

Illustrations
10 Jen Roffe; 70 KJA Artists.

Video
(Florence) © Gurgen Bakhshetsyan/Shutterstock.com; (Bejing) © Assawin/Getty Images; (Cordoba) © wavipicture/Getty Images; (Jeju) © Douglas MacDonald/Getty Images; (Alaska) © Tony Waltham/Getty Images; (Lake Baikal) © Nutexzles/Getty Images; (Rapa Nui/Easter Island) © Jim Richardson/Getty Images; (River Rheine) © Heinz Wohner/LOOK-foto/Getty Images; (Cappadocia) © dziewul/Getty Images; (The Leaning Tower of Pisa) © O. LOUIS MAZZATENTA/National Geographic Creative; (Machu Pichu) © Vladislav T. Jirousek/Shutterstock.com; (Mount Kilimanjaro)© invisiblewl/Getty Images.

Text
We are grateful to the following for permission to reproduce copyright material:
National Geographic for text based on the video Cultural Sensitivity, 5844.flv, http://netpub.ngsp.com/netpub/server.np?find&site=Video_NG_01_PUB&catalog=catalog&template=detail.np&field=itemid&op=matches&value=233521, copyright © 2013, National Geographic Channel. Reproduced with permission; Mr Nicholas Wood for a quotation. Reproduced with kind permission of Mr Nicholas Wood, Political Tours, http://www.politicaltours.com; and Mr James Willcox for a quotation as published in Vacations in Dangerous Places by David Peisner, Departures, 22 August 2012. Reproduced with kind permission of Mr James Willcox, Untamed Borders Ltd, www.untamedborders.com.

Acknowledgements
The publisher and authors would like to thank the following teachers who provided the feedback and user insights on the first edition of Outcomes that have helped us develop this new edition:
Rosetta d'Agostino, New English Teaching, Milan, Italy; Victor Manuel Alarcón, EOI Badalona, Badalona, Spain; Isidro Almendarez, Universidad Complutense, Madrid, Spain; Isabel Andrés, EOI Valdemoro, Madrid, Spain; Brian Brennan, International House Company Training, Barcelona, Spain; Nara Carlini, Università Cattolica, Milan, Italy; Karen Corne, UK; Jordi Dalmau, EOI Reus, Reus, Spain; Matthew Ellman, British Council, Malaysia; Clara Espelt, EOI Maresme, Barcelona, Spain; Abigail Fulbrook, Chiba, Japan; Dylan Gates, Granada, Spain; Blanca Gozalo, EOI Fuenlabrada, Madrid, Spain; James Grant, Japan; Joanna Faith Habershon, St Giles Schools of Languages London Central, UK; Jeanine Hack; English Language Coach.com, London, UK; Claire Hart, Germany; David Hicks, Languages4Life, Barcelona, Spain; Hilary Irving, Central School of English, London, UK; Jessica Jacobs, Università Commerciale Luigi Bocconi, Milan, Italy; Lucia Luciani, Centro di Formaziones Casati, Milan, Italy; Izabela Michalak, ELC, Łódź, Poland; Josep Millanes Moya, FIAC Escola d'Idiomes, Terrassa, Catalonia; Rodrigo Alonso Páramo, EOI Viladecans, Barcelona, Spain; Jonathan Parish, Uxbridge College, London, UK; Mercè Falcó Pegueroles, EOI Tortosa, Tortosa, Spain; Hugh Podmore, St Giles Schools of Languages London Central, UK; James Rock, Università Cattolica, Milan, Italy; Virginia Ron, EOI Rivas, Madrid, Spain; Coletto Russo, British Institutes, Milan, Italy; Ana Salvador, EOI Fuenlabrada, Madrid, Spain; Adam Scott, St Giles College, Brighton, UK; Olga Smolenskaya, Russia; Carla Stroulger, American Language Academy, Madrid, Spain; Simon Thomas, St Giles, UK; Simon Thorley, British Council, Madrid, Spain; Helen Tooke, Università Commerciale Luigi Bocconi, Milan, Italy; Chloe Turner, St Giles Schools of Languages London Central, UK; Sheila Vine, University of Paderborn, Germany; Richard Willmsen, British Study Centres, London, UK; Various teachers at English Studio Academic management, UK.

Authors' acknowledgements
Thanks to Karen Spiller and Katy Wright, and to Dennis Hogan, John McHugh and Gavin McLean for their continued support and enthusiasm.
Thanks also to all the students we've taught over the years for providing more inspiration and insight than they ever realised. And to the colleagues we've taught alongside for their friendship, thoughts and assistance.